Youth Ministry
DRAMA
& COMEDY

Chuck Bolte and Paul McCusker

(Better than bathrobes but not quite Broadway)

Group *Books*

Loveland, Colorado

Youth Ministry Drama & Comedy

Copyright © 1987 by Chuck Bolte and Paul McCusker.

Credits
Edited by Cindy S. Hansen
Cover and book design by Judy Atwood
Cover illustration by Jean Burns and Jan Knudson
Illustrations on pages 47, 48, 49 by Jan Knudson

Library of Congress Cataloging-in-Publication Data
Bolte, Chuck, 1950-
    Youth ministry drama and comedy.

    1. Drama in Christian education.   2. Church work with youth.
I. McCusker, Paul, 1958   II. Title
BV1534.4.B65   1987   246'.7   87-352
ISBN 0931-529-21-2 (pbk.)

18 17 16 15 14 13 12 11 10 9   03 02 01 00 99 98 97 96 95 94

Printed in the United States of America

Dedication

For Paul,
Without whom this book wouldn't
have been possible.
                                    —Chuck

For Chuck,
Likewise, I'm sure.
                    —Paul

And for our mothers
—without whom the above dedication wouldn't have
been possible.

Acknowledgments

W e want to thank Continental Ministries and the many
people who have contributed to Jeremiah People over
the years—not only for their two sketches included in this book,
but for their pioneering efforts in the use of drama and comedy
in the church.

Special thanks to Jim Custer for his work and inspiration.

Thanks to Dave Hoff for allowing us to include "The Christmas
Store" sketch.

Additional gratitude goes to both the "Friday Night Harvest"
and "The Pearly Gates" casts from oh, so long ago; the wonderful folks at Grace Baptist Church in Bowie, Maryland; the ever-
talented group at Calvary Community Church in Thousand Oaks,
California; Pastor Larry DeWitt for his spiritual guidance; Bob
Hoose for always being ready; and Dave Williamson for keeping
the creativity going.

And Chuck still wants to thank Paul who, in return, wants to
thank Chuck. And we still want to thank our mothers.

Contents

PART 1: LEARNING IT

(All About Drama and Comedy)

PART 2: DOING IT

(20 Sketches)

PART 3: FINDING IT

PART 1
LEARNING IT
(All About Drama and Comedy)

An Introduction

(Some Things Are Better Left Unsaid, but We'll Say Them Anyway)

We hope this book is just what the doctor ordered for you. Pushing past all the pretense, technical verbiage and snotty attitudes of "thee-ah-tah" (to be pronounced with nose in the air), we want to give you a fun, "hands-on" approach for organizing a drama and comedy group and putting on a production in your church. We want this to become a book with pages that are dogeared, mangled and written all over. We want this to be a book you'll *use*, not just put on a shelf with the other books you've glanced at and given up as unrealistic. We want to drag drama and comedy kicking and screaming from their lofty heights and put them in your hands where they belong.

We don't care how much or how little experience you have, we believe you can effectively use drama and comedy in your youth ministry and church. We'll give you as many tips and as much information as we can so you can give it your best try.

How Drama and Comedy Help Your Group

Why should you even try to start drama and comedy in your

youth ministry? (A question you'll ask yourself time and time again.) Here are several reasons:

● Drama and comedy are unique ways to get across familiar stories. Flip through some of the sketches in Part 2 that are based on scriptural characters and events such as "Three Witnesses of Pentecost" (see page 201) or "A Phone Call From Elizabeth" (see page 146). As you read the sketches you'll recognize where we got them, but you'll gain a different perspective about the characters and story—which is what drama and comedy are supposed to do.

● Drama and comedy are great opportunities to let your youth group members stretch beyond themselves, trying things they've never done before: work on props, act, develop a character, create a special look with makeup or costumes. You'll be pleasantly surprised at the new interest and unity born out of such a group or production.

● Drama and comedy build kids' confidence and self-esteem. Kids receive positive attention for doing positive things.

● Drama and comedy give youth group members the chance to surprise their family and friends with undiscovered talent.

● Drama and comedy give young people new and unforgettable experiences. They can perform for their own congregation and other churches, or take the production "on the road" for a summer trip. Youth group members can perform plays or sketches that enhance themes for sermons, Bible studies and fellowship events.

● Youth group members will develop teamwork and group cohesiveness by working on a production. They'll have to. You can't get involved emotionally in a sketch or production without being affected by the people around you.

● Kids can step out of their own "youth group member" role and be whomever they want to be: a pastor, a protective father, a gossip, a counselor, Martin Luther, John the Baptist's mother, a hero, a villain, a nerd. The possibilities are limited only by imagination.

● Drama and comedy provide ways for kids to discover, expand and use their creative abilities.

Got the idea?

How Can This Book Help Me Start Drama and Comedy With My Kids?

We've done our best to make *Youth Ministry Drama and Comedy* as practical as possible—it's a "roll-up-your-sleeves-and-dig-in" approach. Part 1 covers a wide variety of topics you'll need to know to start drama and comedy in your youth group. You'll learn about the background of drama and comedy in the church and how they got to where they are today. You'll also learn how to:

- decide what type of production is best for your specific situation;
- determine goals and a budget;
- choose the right script, or write your own;
- audition kids for parts;
- run rehearsals;
- direct the production from beginning to end;
- understand acting terms such as stage right, stage left, blocking, etc.;
- work with lighting, sound, props, sets, makeup, costumes;
- decide how many or how few props, costumes and "extra touches" you'll need for your production.

Part 2 includes 20 scripts that cover topics such as Bible study, Bible characters, Christmas, confidentiality, dating, parent-child relationships, role of the pastor, listening, love, reconciliation, Pentecost, complaining and generosity. Each sketch includes several discussion questions you can ask your actors or audience to get them to think more deeply about the sketch's message. You can copy the scripts for use in your immediate youth group. However, if another church wants to perform the sketches, it must purchase a copy of the book in order to receive performance rights (Group Books, Box 481, Loveland, CO 80539).

Part 3 lists many resources you may find helpful. You'll find titles of plays you can use, addresses of drama organizations and book clubs, and companies where you can inquire about all your drama needs such as lighting, makeup, costumes, sound and sets. Most important, you'll find a list of exceptional works by one of the authors (and his name is *not* Chuck Bolte . . . ahem).

As you read this book, keep in mind our only philosophical viewpoint: If you want to start drama and comedy in the church, just *do it*. Your biggest battles will involve balances. You'll have to balance the message against the medium (or good theatrical technique), goals against guesswork, purpose against performance, your desire to be expressive against your audience's expectations, creativity against communication.

Certain preachers will argue, various artists will disagree, you might even find yourself rethinking certain things—we'll leave that to you. But we believe that the most satisfying production (for you and your audience) will be the one that keeps the scales right in the center, achieving the best on all sides.

Balance. It's all a matter of balance. A word that you'll see more and more as you read this book.

Get On With It, Will You?

Okay, that's it. We're going to tackle as much as we can with as little confusion as possible. Are you ready? Please, step this way . . .

1
Background of Drama and Comedy

(The Here and Now of the Way Back When)

Every book has to start somewhere and this one may as well start at the beginning. Not the beginning of drama and comedy, per se, but some perspectives about drama and comedy, what they are and how they got to where they are today—especially in the church.

What makes this chapter important is that it can help you convince leading skeptics that your desire for drama and comedy in the church isn't merely a whim on your part but an ongoing progression in a larger, scriptural and historical scheme of eternity. (The skeptics won't understand what you're talking about, but they'll be impressed with the thought behind it.) In other words, if the skeptics will give you a chance, drama and comedy could prove to be "good things." (Oh, *that's* what that means.)

If you've won over the skeptics and know as much as you need to know about drama and comedy, then move on to the next chapter. Otherwise, do not pass "Go," do not collect $200, and indulge us for a few pages. (Purists beware. We won't be taking conventional routes to get to our answers.)

A Biblical Base for Drama and Comedy

We won't kid you on this. If you're looking for a direct scripture verse that says something like: "And he went among his kindred, performing drama and comedy to the glorification of the Lord, and the blessings of the multitudes were upon him" (1 Opinions 2:3), forget it. Such a verse doesn't exist. But that doesn't mean drama and comedy are somehow unscriptural. Fact is: The Bible is full of drama and comedy. Have you read the book of Esther recently? Or the account of the rise and fall of Saul and David? All of the elements of good drama and comedy can be found there in the humanity, failures, ironic twists, victories, betrayals, love, bitterness and celebrations. (These Bible stories could have been the scripts for night-time soap operas.) It's no wonder the Bible is constantly used for stage and screen—through literal adaptation, allusion, symbolic reference or blatant plagiarism. It's perfect for them.

But let's take this one subject at a time, if only to clarify our terms.

Humor and Comedy

Let's consider humor and comedy. (It isn't that we get paid by the word, we just want to make sure we're all thinking the same things.)

Humor is an attitude, a disposition. Comedy is a theatrical term that uses humor. The two terms are related but distinct.

Humor is a vital part of our human existence. Practical experience shows that good humor is healthy. It relieves tension, creates better circulation, heals certain physical ailments, and might even be a cure for acne. (It's hard for those little red bandits to sprout when a face is contorted with laughter—but don't quote us on it.) A gentleman by the name of Norman Cousins claims that in the face of a serious illness, he laughed himself back to health.

Humor and its subsequent theatrical form of comedy break down communication barriers. The most skillful communicators, writers, politicians, salespeople and pastors know to use humor and comedy to make the listener more receptive to their message or idea. The effective use of humor and comedy creates an atmosphere of openness designed to disarm you so you'll be more inclined to accept what's being said.

Let's face it—we like people who make us laugh. They make

us feel comfortable. Somehow they keep life from being too burdensome. They lift our spirits and encourage us. We want to be around them. Do you know why? Because humor gives us a sense of hope. And people who have a sense of humor create an atmosphere that makes us realize things just "ain't so bad" as they might seem.

Think about the people you know who laugh and can make you laugh. Now think about those who don't. Whom would you rather be with?

A basic fact is that few of us trust people who never laugh. Then again, few of us trust people who laugh all the time. Which is to say that humor and comedy, like most things in life, must be a matter of balance. (But more about that later.)

Drama and Comedy in the Bible

Take a close look at some of the psalms and proverbs in the Bible. You won't find the same type of one-liners or wit we're accustomed to today, but you will find humor. Solomon, for all of the moroseness of Ecclesiastes, turns around in Proverbs with his tongue firmly implanted in his cheek (or wisdom tooth) and presents a very ironic look at humanity and God. (This example is correct if Solomon did write all of Ecclesiastes and Proverbs. If he didn't, it was probably because he was too busy keeping track of all his wives and concubines. Just kidding.)

Consider the imagery used in most of the Psalms. For example, look at Psalms 58, 102 and 143. The richness of the language, the power of emotions—from anger, to joy, to self-deprecating humor—all work to create poetic scenes of drama and comedy.

Do you think David and the other psalmists were people who didn't laugh occasionally, even at their own misfortune? They could afford to laugh. They had God on their side. As believers, so do we.

Or, as a more classic example, consider the words of Jesus in the Sermon on the Mount. Not that Jesus was some kind of stand-up comedian, but he certainly knew the value of a good turn of phrase or absurd image. Picture the expression he uses in Matthew 7:3-5 in which Jesus tells the listeners to take the logs out of their own eyes before they try to take the speck out of someone else's.

Imagine that command literally and you get a very funny picture. Not that the disciples were rolling on the ground doubled up with laughter. They probably weren't. The Pharisees certainly weren't. But it's a good example of Jesus' use of absurdist humor—the hyperbole. Straining out a gnat and swallowing a camel (Matthew 23:24), or getting a camel through the eye of a needle (Luke 18:25) are other examples.

Types of Comedy

This brings us, then, to simplified explanations of the types of comedy often associated with theatre and other forms of communication.

One is *non-statement comedy* or what some texts call *low comedy* (as a descriptive term, not qualitative). This type of comedy has no purpose other than to make you laugh. As often as possible. There are different manifestations of this sort of comedy: slapstick, vaudeville, burlesque, some of the situation comedies on television, and many of today's teen movies. (We'd give you a list of these movies, but that would imply we've seen them, heaven forbid.) The humor of non-statement comedy is physical, heavy-handed, obvious, and appealing to the "gut" rather than the intellect. Non-statement comedy is to the stage what junk food is to the stomach—fun and tasty, but devoid of any nourishment.

In and of itself, there is nothing wrong with this type of humor depending on how it's used. It can be successfully used for youth group crowdbreakers and "just for fun" at different church activities. Sometimes it's good to laugh for the sake of laughter alone. But trying to build a church theatre group around this kind of comedy alone would be a mistake. You might keep your audiences laughing for a while but the lack of substance will ultimately betray you. Eat nothing but chocolate for a couple of weeks and see if your constitution doesn't rebel.

The other type of comedy is (as if you couldn't guess) *statement comedy* or *high comedy*—referring again to the more official terminology. This comedy takes a more intellectual approach. It conveys a message to the mind and heart. Behind the laughter it creates, it shows us (through subtlety, irony, absurdity and farce) the quirks and foibles of our society and, within the church, our spirituality. And because we want to simplify as much as possible, we'll lump high comedy under the word *satire*.

Note that we said *satire*—which we do not want to be confused with *sarcasm*. Let's take a look at the differences between satire and sarcasm according to the Chuck Bolte and Paul McCusker School of Semantics. (Purists are really going to start protesting now.)

By strict definition, satire and sarcasm are very similar. Both can involve sneering, mocking, biting, scathing, ridiculing, attacking, deriding, and being caustic to a person or organization.

Side-stepping the strict definition, though, we want to clarify the primary differences between the two terms. (Be patient. We may be destroying the English language but we're doing it with good intentions.)

The primary differences between sarcasm and satire are purpose and outcome. Sarcasm's only purpose is to sneer, mock, bite, scathe, ridicule, attack, deride, and be caustic in order to hurt the organization or person to whom those things are directed. It's a sharp stick designed to poke fatal holes. It's bone-breaking for the sake of crippling. (This is the "mix-and-match" approach to metaphors.) The outcome? That person or organization is . . . well, *hurt*. No more and no less.

Sarcasm can be funny, no question about it. Certain comedians are making fortunes in Las Vegas using this sort of humor. And we laugh—even when it's directed at us—for a while. But only for a while. And then sarcasm wears thin and stops being funny. It becomes pointless (much like non-statement humor's effect after a time) and bears no constructive value. Then, when all is said and done, we realize we've been left with nothing . . . but the hurt.

Probably one of the more common places for sarcasm to raise its pointed and ugly little head is in youth groups. (Oh, *really?*) Deriding comments about people's physical appearance, dress, voice, circle of friends, etc. are commonplace even among the most spiritual of youth groups (or adult groups for that matter). Specific premeditated intent to hurt is not always at the heart of sarcasm; but the destructive, disunifying outcome is always the same.

Satire, on the other hand, has some of the characteristics of sarcasm but the purpose and outcome change. The purpose is to point out folly, ignorance, error, or merely to get people or organizations to look inward about an attitude or action. The outcome, if it is done right, is to have the people or organizations laughing and then—bingo—they suddenly realize at whom they're laughing.

Themselves.

It's the "Ha, ha, *ouch*" effect. Satire is a sharp stick with healing salve on the end. It's bone-breaking for the sake of resetting to create stronger limbs (and build strong bodies 12 ways). The prophet Jeremiah understood this. His ministry was one of tearing down in order to build up.

In the church, satire can be one of the most effective ways to get a message across for the reason we've mentioned before: Laughter breaks down our guard and makes us more open to ideas we might otherwise dispute.

There's a thin line between sarcasm and satire. One can easily masquerade as the other—at least, until the outcome. Then it becomes clear what it is. Sarcasm or satire is unmasked. If you're attempting a production with the intent of using satire but your audience feels like you've unloaded a lot of sarcasm on them, then you better look carefully at what you're doing. (Which is why we emphasize both purpose and outcome. What you intend to do and what the outcome proves to be are often two very separate things.)

Thus, having beaten our semantics within inches of its life, we move on.

Drama and Its Use in the Church

Coming up with a concise discussion of drama is difficult and best suited for verbose texts dedicated strictly to that subject. It's like discussing music. There are numerous forms and styles and each one can fuse with another. And whatever you try to do with music (or drama), you're going to step on somebody's taste buds. (Or should that be "somebody's toes"?) You need to get used to this reaction. Your entire experience with church "creative arts" will involve this problem. Just ask any music minister.

Simply stated: Drama is a serious approach to human issues and conflicts. It can incorporate certain elements of comedy but, for the most part, doesn't. Drama can be straightforward, symbolic, parabolic, almost anything.

As in our discussion of comedy, drama in the church must communicate a message or truth. Drama merely for the sake of drama can be all right in some circumstances, but if it remains spiritually void your church leadership will probably shut you down. And so they should. Why bother using church time and money for something that won't challenge or edify believers or bring outsiders into your assembly? (Is that a utilitarian viewpoint or what? Deal with it.)

The main consideration for using drama in the church is: What type of drama is most appropriate for your audience? What type of drama will get the message across to them? Should it be a tragedy? straight drama? melodrama? fantasy? What style should be used? Something realistic? abstract? impressionistic? romantic? Some of these decisions will be made as you select material, or will be made for you by the material you select.

The key is to be sensitive to what type of drama will work for your particular audience. We've said it before and we'll say it again: Your production won't be worth anything if it doesn't communicate effectively to your audience. Sure, you can be creative and experimental, but within the boundaries of your audience's ability to take in what you're trying to do. They're not a bunch of dolts, but they might not be on your same wavelength. Always consider that fact.

The other side of the issue is not to box yourself in too much. The biggest problem with typical church drama today is just that: It is typical church drama.

Somebody somewhere decided that to be considered church drama, it must be overwritten to become a blunt instrument and overacted to ensure that the audience is beaten senseless with the point.

Wrong.

Somebody somewhere decided that to be considered church drama, it must be like Shakespeare.

Wrong.

Somebody somewhere decided that to be considered church drama, it must include biblical characters and a cast dressed in bathrobes speaking King James Version English. (And it can only be seen seasonally.)

Wrong. (Wrong.)

Who are these somebodies, and where are they making these decisions? They be us, folks. And they're right under our noses.

A Brief History of Church Drama

There are reasons for such attitudes about church drama, but don't expect to hear all of them. The Reader's Digress Condensed Version might go something like this:

See, once upon a time a few hundred years ago (not counting daylight-saving time), drama was embraced by the church and nurtured there. It was incorporated into services and displayed in courtyards. Drama actually carried a certain degree of excellence in message and medium. But theatre in the secular realm began to taint it. Actors and actresses often doubled as prostitutes, and the stage became a place for messages that proved . . . well, less than Christian. And as often happens with royalty and religion, assorted leadership didn't approve of views that didn't agree with their own (scriptural or not). Blasphemies, boycotts, banishments, and the overall reputation of the theatre (and people associated with it) finally made most churches give up on it.

Does that "condensed version" sound familiar? Think of our own century with all the technological advancements in communication and how many mainstream churches have dealt with those advancements. Think of motion pictures, television and certain styles of music. Due to sin by association, churches have been slow to use what has been developed—attributing good and evil to such things because of the world's abuses. However, technological advancements are not inherently good or evil but simply neutral tools. And when we do decide to use them, the results are often amateurish, crass and void of any style or grace.

Drama remains in this category.

So What's the Problem?

We have several theories why such problems exist. One is the attitude that anything secular must be completely and thoroughly bad and should be shunned. We can't argue with such a viewpoint (it automatically shuts out any discussion).

Another more moderate view is that certain forms of communication really aren't "of the devil" but don't you dare tell us how to use them properly. How dare you suggest that Christian motion pictures and television could benefit from good camera technique or scripting! How dare you tell us that some basics in acting might help, or that a certain production trick might make our music sound better! Heaven forbid that we should learn from our secular counterparts in areas of technique. (Of course, if Christian physicians took this same attitude we'd have no Christian physicians. We'd still be bloodletting to get rid of disease and putting heads in vises to cure headaches.)

The opposite extreme to this reasoning is our current fascination for "Christianizing" secular successes; our marketers realizing that if it made lots of money over there then we should put a Christian tag on it and try it over here. Sadly enough we, as consumers, are going along with it.

But enough of the soapbox delivery.

Another theory why church drama can be so bad is because we're trying too hard to get our message across. In our enthusiasm to preach, we forget to apply basic rules of good theatre (or communication). God will often use such productions to his glory in spite of themselves. But think of what God could have done if both message and medium were at their best!

Another theory why church drama can be so bad is that some church drama is lopsided on the production end and too light on the message end.

Balance. It's all a matter of balance.

Yet another theory about the problems with church drama is simply one of perception. While we think that comedy is fairly easy to pull off (a terrible misconception), we're intimidated by what we think of as drama. When we think of drama, we think of Shakespeare, O'Neill, meaningful dialogue, character analysis, and all the things we hated in high school. And, in the face of such an overwhelming perception, we quit before we get started.

Oh, but we have to do something, so we go with a program that everyone knows and will accept. And there we are once again, standing on stage in bathrobes, pointing to a papier-mâché rock with expressions of shock and surprise, while an angel in white bed sheets and cardboard wings tells us, "He is not here. He has risen." And everyone in the audience smiles and nods and will tell us how much the production meant to them. And we'll smile back through gritted teeth, because we knew we could have (and should have) done something better.

Maybe next time.

So What Are We Waiting For?

Drama and comedy can—and do—have a significant impact on our emotional, physical, social and spiritual lives. One way or another, through television, motion pictures, radio and stage, we're being influenced and affected. We can easily forget a sermon or lecture, but we're not so quick to forget good drama and comedy.

It seems inconceivable that we have such communicative power available to the church but haven't been using it. What are we waiting for?

Keep reading before you answer that question.

2
Developing Goals and a Budget

(What Shall It Be, and Who's Going to Pay for It?)

Before we wrote a single word for this book, we sat down and carefully developed a "statement of purpose." We considered who the audience would be, the content, style, format, and two or three other ideals. Once we established our statement of purpose, we sent it to our editor. With his input, we clarified it even more. From there, we developed a general outline of each chapter. After the outline was approved, we began the actual writing.

Had we skipped those early procedures, we might have saved time and had a book on the market sooner, but there's no telling what the book would have been like. The book could have started off dealing with drama and comedy in youth ministry and the church, and wandered into a discussion of improving your golf swing, 101 uses for bellybutton lint, or how to raise sugar beets in Minnesota. The point is: Anything of reasonable importance must be the result of specific goals and proper planning.

In other words, before you try to do any drama and comedy with your youth group, you better have a good idea of what you're trying to accomplish. Otherwise, your good idea could become a Frankenstein's monster—killing the maker, destroying the village and creating a whole series of terrible films. (Draining you and your church of time, energy and resources.)

If you want to get started with drama and comedy, and you want to avoid creating a Frankenstein's monster, answer the questions found at the end of this chapter. The answers to these questions help you set goals for your production. They also help you determine costs that may affect your budget. If you don't answer these questions, you'll find yourself frustrated. Trust us. Your group will be confused, your church leaders will question your salvation, and your congregation will ask you to return the key to the executive washroom.

None of this is to say that your early goals and planning can't be modified as you progress. They can. You'll find several unexpected twists and turns in the direction your group takes. Be flexible. But no matter what happens, you can fall back on your initial foundation of goals.

This Ain't Broadway

Be realistic with your goals. This ain't Broadway. Too many churches decide to start a drama and comedy group, throw everything they have into an extravagant production, and then—if the production flops—believe that it was God's way of telling them never to do drama and comedy again.

If you're just beginning, start small and see how it grows. Give yourself room to learn, adapt and make mistakes—but on a minimal scale. Start by using short sketches in a variety of situations such as services, activities and banquets. If the short sketches are successful, then combine the sketches with music and put on a variety show. From there, try a one-act play. Then possibly a full-length play. Then maybe a musical or dinner theatre. And from there . . . anything can happen.

But whatever you do, don't be guilty of jumping too far ahead of yourself (or your church) with grandiose visions of elaborate costumes, intricate lights and sound, or enormous sets. Chances are, it'll backlash in a number of horrible-and-too-gruesome-to-describe ways.

The Buck Stops Where?

After you develop your goals, and you want to get some degree of approval from the church leadership, one question will certainly raise its ugly head. Yes, beyond your vision, beyond the benefits for everyone everywhere, and beyond the larger, scriptural and historical scheme of eternity, someone is going to ask: "What will the production cost us?"

If you've planned properly, you'll be able to tell them. Confidently, you'll smile and explain that it won't cost much to perform short sketches. You'll use two chairs to represent a living room and regular clothes for the costumes. The technical facilities in the church will fill your needs for a stage, sound and lights. (Okay, maybe you might have to rent a couple of things but it isn't such a terrible expense considering what some churches are doing.) And you'll sound very sane. And you'll sound very reasonable. And you'll probably get the money you need.

The other, more typical, scenario would be offering the church leadership a long list of materials, sets, lights, microphones, electricity, facilities, and time you'll need to put together something akin to a Cecil B. De Mille film. They might go for it through your powers of persuasion or their own personal visions. But if the production bombs . . . don't say we didn't warn you.

Thus, we return to what we just finished saying: Be realistic with your goals. Most churches don't look too kindly on what appears to be wasted money. So, as you decide on your goals and develop your budget, keep in mind two things:

1. Work with your church leadership. Don't take the role of adversary even if you run up against skeptics and resistance. Drama and comedy in the church are still fairly new to most people, and you'll need all your diplomatic powers to persuade people of the importance of theatre. This is especially true in matters regarding money. Maintain a spirit of cooperation (even when the stereotypical "artistic temperament" would tell you otherwise). A spirit of cooperation will help in the second thing you need to remember.

2. Like it or not, your drama and comedy group will have to prove itself. From the very first minute of its existence, you'll have to establish credibility with your leadership, congregation and even those in your group. This is true in the area of money as well as in the types of productions you do (choice of scripts, content, topics and other things we'll cover in later chapters). Every step of the way, you'll be working to legitimize what you're doing so that everyone will see it's not just an artistic whim, an extravagant idea or self-indulgent scheme. Don't let your own enthusiasm and expectations blind you to the fact that not everyone will be as dedicated or as involved as you are. (Like the times you'll want to rehearse and three of your cast members have a church softball game. Or the room in which you need to rehearse has been rescheduled for someone else's meeting. Or . . . the situations go on and on.) These people are still watching and waiting to see if the group will really make it.

If you remember this point and act accordingly, people will be more inclined to support you in your next project.

You may ask, "If I produce consistent successes, will I ever have full cooperation and credibility?"

Probably not. Oh, you'll gain some cooperation and credibility, but never what you think you deserve. The "creative arts" ministries are always subjected to the most scrutiny and skepticism. "You're only as good as your last hit" is a secular maxim but applicable to the Christian realm as well.

If your plans are met with skepticism, don't be discouraged or paranoid or pull the "creative wagons" in a circle. Don't encourage an "us-against-them, they-just-don't-understand-art" mentality. Remember the first point. Work hard and diplomatically with your church leadership to get the support you need. Then if you constantly run up against opposition, you should either double-check what you're doing or realize that your church isn't ready for this sort of ministry.

Okay, Okay . . . I Still Don't Know Where to Start

Honest, we really don't get paid by the word. We just want you to understand fully what to expect. So relax for 30 seconds . . .

Time's up.

Now, here are questions to ponder while you're setting your goals and, especially, while you're establishing your budget. (We'll be covering many of these areas in later chapters so don't panic. We're listing them here simply to have them in one convenient place.)

1. What is the purpose of this specific production? the overall group?

2. What spiritual and emotional aspects would we like to see within the cast? production crew?

3. Who is the audience? Are they congregation members?

other Christians? the community? non-believers?

4. What are we trying to accomplish with our audience?

5. Will our drama and comedy group work through the church, or will our primary focus be external? (For example, "on the road" and evangelistic.)

6. What will we perform? Will it be a short sketch? full-length play? musical? dinner theatre? one-act play?

7. Will our script be original, or will we use something published? If published, how much will it cost to buy or rent the appropriate number of copies? (Thou shalt not make thine own copies of a published work without permission regardless of previous practice or what anyone tells you. Argue the legality but the fact is: It's not ethical.) Will there be performance fees involved? Sometimes publishers charge performance fees above and beyond the cost of the scripts.

8. Who will direct?

9. Will the group lead workshops to help cultivate acting abilities and creative talent? Or will the group simply provide an alternative for those who can't sing in the youth choir?

10. Will we perform in the church sanctuary or at another site? Will we have to pay a rental fee?

11. Will someone set up the auditorium (seats, etc.) for us, or will we have to do it ourselves? Who will clean up after the performance?

12. When and how often will we perform?

13. Where and how often will we rehearse? How can we balance rehearsal schedules with other youth ministry and school activities?

14. Will we cast strictly from within the youth group? the entire church? Or should we open it up to other people in the community?

15. What technical assistance do we need? Who will be responsible for costumes? lights? sound? sets? multimedia? What additional items are needed? How much will they cost to buy or rent?

16. Do we want to incorporate music? If so, will it be performed live or on tape? If live, who will play it? If taped, where will we get the tape? Is the music copyrighted, and will we have to pay a fee to perform it?

17. What kind of publicity do we want? Should we use press releases? posters? fliers? Who will be in charge of publicity?

18. Based on our church beliefs, should we charge admission or take a freewill offering? In either case, should we distribute tickets? If so, who will be in charge? Should we distribute tickets through various outlets? through the mail? by phone? at the door? How much should we charge for the tickets?

19. Will there be child care the night of the performance(s)? ushers?

20. What are anticipated miscellaneous expenditures? (Try to think of everything. This is a category that'll sneak up on you during the production.) As you're putting together your budget, avoid guessing at expenses that you don't really know about. Take the time to find out from someone who does know. (Don't be guilty of "Oh, a friend of mine was positive it would cost such and such.") Make a few phone calls to be sure of prices.

Once you get started, you'll think of more questions since every church has its own unique set of circumstances. But don't let them intimidate you. Many of these questions will be answered in a "domino" fashion. (As you answer one question, it'll fall onto the next and be answered as well). And don't be lazy. It's better to ask all of these questions before you start than find yourself struggling with them in the middle—when it's too late to answer them correctly.

Okay, now let's roll up our sleeves and dig into some of the details about starting drama and comedy in your youth ministry.

3
Choosing or Writing Scripts

(Putting the Words in Their Mouths)

Take a ride to your friendly neighborhood Christian gift emporium. Move past the wall of better-way-to-do-it best sellers, the latest videos from your favorite artists, the charismatic cards for all occasions, the evangelistic buttons, blessed bumper stickers and scripture key chains, the believer's aerobics display, and the rack of romance novels for the righteous, and you might meet a pleasant individual who'll ask if he or she can help you in some way. You'll nod and ask, "Do you have any books about drama and comedy in the church?"

The pleasant individual will look at you quizzically and ask, "I beg your pardon?"

"You know, skits and plays? Performed on a stage?"

The pleasant individual will scratch his or her chin, shrug and say, "I don't think we carry anything like that, but I'll show you what we have."

And in some dusty corner you'll find a children's musical left over from Christmas, a book of discussion-starter skits for youth groups (copyrighted 1954), and a short Easter dramatization of the Last Supper.

A Little Background (Oh No, Not Again)

A lot of people complain that they want to do drama and comedy in their church but can't find the material. A lot of the Christian publishers complain that they want to publish drama and comedy for the church but can't sell the material. It's a typical Catch-22 situation.

Both sides are absolutely correct, and the resolution isn't going to be easy. Somebody has to make the first move. Either people will have to push ahead and make use of the material available to assure the publishers that there really is a market, or the publishers will have to go out on a financial limb and begin ''experimenting'' with different forms of drama and comedy to convince people that there really *is* such a thing as good Christian drama and comedy. (Long sentence, eh?)

The market isn't completely barren, however. There are good resources available if you know where to look. (And we'll help you as much as we can in the resource section of this book.) Unfortunately, though, most of the market is exactly what you've come to expect. Finding the right material is tough no matter what you do. But knowing what to look for will help limit the amount of wasted time.

Let's talk about that.

What Scripts to Look For

Before you begin your search for material, you must have some idea of what you're looking for. Your church (or youth group) is unique, with specific needs and goals. Whatever you do should address these needs and goals. You have to be aware of your audience. (We can't say it enough.) Don't get so lost in your own vision of what you or your group wants to do that you forget the message you're trying to communicate or to whom it's being communicated.

Beyond sheer entertainment value, pinpoint an area or topic that would be meaningful to your young people. Choose material that complements a sermon series by your pastor, or material that addresses the overall concerns or struggles your kids might be having. If you're using drama and comedy to communicate truth, then you must remain sensitive to what truth needs to be communicated.

This doesn't give you license to use drama and comedy as

weapons for attack or forums for your personal gripes against your church or some of its members. To do so would betray any degree of credibility you might have established in addition to causing some people to look at you with ill humor.

Another thing to look for is a script that won't be too difficult to understand, yet won't insult the audience's intelligence. Look for material that explains enough for the audience to follow along but leaves out enough so they'll have something to think about. (T.S. Eliot once said, "A play should give you something to think about. When I see a play and understand it the first time, then I know it can't be much good." Food for thought.) Sound like a tall order? It is. But, only you can determine your audience's level of sophistication.

So, when you start looking for material—whether it's comedy or drama—choose a script with a prayerful and sensitive heart toward the needs of your audience.

And this is where we come full circle again. (Good grief, what now?) Yeah, it's the old balance issue. The best script will insightfully address topics and issues of humanity and Christianity, getting the message across without sacrificing good principles of drama and comedy. It's the balance between message and medium that we continue to talk about.

Equal to that, choose a script that is well-written in terms of the fundamentals of good drama and comedy: story, plot, character, language and idea.

What Scripts to Stay Away From

Still not enough to help you? Well, then, let's look at a few of the negatives (since there seem to be more of those in Christian scripts than positives). The types of scripts to stay away from:

1. Scripts that lack subtlety. This is a prime complaint we have with a majority of Christian scripts. In fact, all of the following paragraphs are variations of this point. (Not that we're trying to be repetitious, but there are degrees of this offense. Be careful of them all.)

2. Scripts that use characters and dialogue which are merely vehicles to preach a message. Such scripts are "commercials for Christ" with all the depth and dimension of two Madison Avenue creations selling soap powder. ("Ring around the lifestyle? Wash those dirty rings out with Christianity!" Wink,

wink. Nudge, nudge.) How embarrassing.

3. Scripts that preach about specific behavior. Too many Christian scripts get lost in personal "doctrines of lifestyle" rather than the truth of scripture and how it applies to the human condition. Good drama and comedy explore the topics related to—and the attitudes behind—our actions as both human beings and Christians. Scripts don't need to deal solely with the right or wrong of "smoking, drinking, chewing, spitting, drugs, sex and rock 'n roll." Good scripts should deal with the inner workings of the character's spirit and soul that might lead him or her to rebel against God, and the other inner workings that bring him or her back into fellowship with God.

Does that mean Christian scripts shouldn't take a stand about certain contemporary issues and problems? Of course they should. But be careful whose stand the scripts are taking. Having a "theatrical finger" shaken at the audience about the "gray areas" will likely alienate them more quickly than standing and reprimanding them face to face. Apart from disagreeing with you, they might resent being told what to do. You would too, wouldn't you?

4. Scripts that reduce characters to good guys (Christians) and bad guys (non-Christians). In real life, we're a little of both. Christians aren't always right in what they do and say, and non-Christians aren't always wrong in what they do and say. (The only exception to this might be a comedic spoof of some sort.) Even the Bible gives us balanced portraits of its heroes and saints. Why shouldn't our stage productions?

5. Scripts that exploit or sensationalize current topics, trends or issues. All topics are to be handled sensitively, not blown out of proportion for the sake of a message.

6. Scripts that try to do everything. We recently stumbled across a sketch that dealt with faith, life after death, a visitation by an angel, prayer, Christian hypocrisy, a philosophical argument about the existence of God, God's intervention in human affairs (Why does he let evil persist?), conversion, the horror of war, and healing . . . all in seven pages. Needless to say, it didn't work.

But these are only a few suggestions about what to watch out for when searching for material. You'll discern even more as you begin . . .

Reading Scripts for Yourself

The only way you're going to make a sound, intelligent decision about which material to choose is by reading a lot of scripts—both Christian and secular.

What?!

Yes, you read right. We don't want you to compromise any convictions, but we'd hate for you to limit yourself. There's a lot to be said for looking at the "other side." Only as you become well-versed in different forms and styles of playwriting will you know what material will work for you.

But don't think reading a script is the same as reading a novel or non-fiction book. Unlike most forms of literature, a script is not complete on the page. It's just an outline or representation of what it's supposed to be. Sure, you'll see all the character's names and their lines and where they're supposed to be and hints at how they'll move, but so many more details must be filled in by the director, actors, sets and costumes. Try to visualize these things as you read a script.

To broaden your knowledge of good scripts, contact some of the publishing companies listed in the resource section of this book. Order free catalogs and possibly even "reading copies" of some of their offerings. If you're really serious about this, we also recommend that you join a book club such as the "Fireside Theatre," which offers both contemporary and classic plays in both hard-cover and soft-cover at very reasonable prices. (Fireside Theatre is also listed in the resource section.) Look in the resource section for a list of plays worth reading. Not because they're the best plays ever written, but because they represent a wide spectrum of the plays that are available. If you don't want to buy them, you can always check them out at your local library.

Bringing the Scripts Back Home

The truth is: You can read all the plays you want but can you do them? Lack of time, talent, and experience could inhibit you and your group from doing the one you'd like to do.

You must constantly ask yourself a number of important questions:

- Will the script help the cast and crew grow in faith?
- Does the script fit our goals? (For example, if one of the

goals is to take the production on the road, choose a simple sketch that requires minimum props. Or if one of the goals is to enhance a Bible study, meeting topic, retreat theme or sermon, choose an appropriate script that will accomplish that goal.)

- Do we really understand the play well enough to perform it?
- Do we have the facilities?
- Do we have the actors who will do the characters justice?
- Do we need other technical resources, or can the play or sketch be done with what we have (and still maintain quality)?
- Do we have the people to help with costumes and other "behind-the-scenes" jobs?

As with our discussion of the budget, all of these questions and more must be answered before a play can be selected.

Making Changes in the Script to Suit Your Needs

As a general rule: Don't change the script. For one thing, changes might infringe on the author's copyright. For another thing, you could seriously damage the play itself. Some respect for the author and his or her intentions must be maintained. Changing or omitting lines, portions of plot, or characters might unintentionally destroy the very things for which you chose the play.

But what happens if the play comes extremely close to your needs and would be "absolutely perfect" if a few changes were made? Well . . . then a few careful alterations might be permissible (providing the author or publisher hasn't stated that such alterations would be breaking the law).

For instance, it is generally permissible to change words or phrases that might prove offensive or confusing to your particular audience. Older plays or plays that take place in a strange locale might cause problems by virtue of different meanings, dated expressions or unfamiliar phrasings. Another instance might be condensing the sets in a play that has more than you can handle.

Apart from those instances, we highly advise that you leave the work alone. The temptation is to think that, as director or actor, you can do a better job than the author. Sometimes that might be true. But true or not, you must defer to the ability of the author to have articulated what he or she meant through characters and dialogue. It's not your place to improve on the author's work—especially without his or her approval. It just ain't the right thing to do.

Do we sound a little overly sensitive about this? Well, forgive us if we do. But be assured that if you change anything in this book, you'll be hearing from our lawyers (from the illustrious law firm of Bruno, Knuckles, Ripper and Distemper).

Rights and Permission

Most secular plays involve some sort of production/performance fee beyond the cost of the individual copies. Generally, such a fee is listed in the front of the play or can be obtained from the publisher. Fees vary from play to play, depending upon such things as author and popularity, etc. Fees also can vary from Broadway plays to Broadway musicals.

Some of the Christian plays also have production/performance fees, though not quite as high-priced. You need to be aware of these costs for budget purposes, and to give us an excuse to warn you not to shrug off this responsibility. Please, don't even consider the "financial shortcut" of buying one script and then duplicating it for your cast and crew. It's not legal and it's certainly not ethical.

One editor for a secular play publishing house that has a religious line recently lamented that of all the high schools, colleges, amateur and community theatre groups, and general buyers, churches are the worst offenders for not paying production/performance fees and for illegally duplicating scripts. Great testimony, huh?

There are a lot of excuses about for this. Some are even understandable. "My church simply can't afford it" or, "It's not their work, it belongs to God and we must share freely" or, "The copyright laws are vague about it because we're non-profit" or, well, you've heard all the excuses. Maybe you've even used a few of them.

The reality is this: If you want quality Christian material, then somebody has to write it. The only way anyone can and will write it is if he or she can make enough money to live on. By shirking the appropriate fees or duplicating books, you are taking away from the writer's livelihood. And you know what happens? That person has to quit in order to find another vocation to pay the bills. And then we're right back at the dilemma found at the beginning of this chapter. (Pretty handy how that worked out, huh?)

What If I Want to Write a Script Myself?

Creating your own short sketches or longer plays is certainly a viable alternative. You might surprise yourself. One author began writing scripts for his church out of necessity and never stopped. Many of his sketches are published and he's now writing scripts professionally. As was true for him, doing it yourself may be your only choice. The demand for sketches that meet your church's unique needs may make it impossible to find anything in the marketplace. What should you do?

Though we can't teach you how to write—at least, not in this small amount of space—we can give you some suggestions about writing scripts yourself or as a group.

● If you think you have even an inkling of ability to write, sit down and do it.

● Check published scripts for format ideas and then begin.

● No more excuses.

● Think about what you want to say, how to say it, and the characters and situations that will bring it to life.

● Don't expect to be Shakespeare.

● Take writing courses.

● Read some of the more extensive books about writing scripts.

● But whatever you do, don't just sit there thinking about it anymore. Start!

We've already established the need for more Christian playwriters—you could be one of them. (Sounds like one of those magazine ads: "Draw Blinky and become a successful artist!")

The Corporate Approach to Writing Scripts

Creating your own scripts as a group effort can be a lot of fun if you follow some very basic suggestions.

1. Meet in a setting that is comfortable and away from distractions. If possible, assemble all interested people in a circle. Give them pads of paper and pens, and keep a tape recorder running. Also make room for some improvisation. (Improvisation, if you don't know, is a technique that lets any number of people act out freely and spontaneously an imaginary situation. More about it later.)

2. Every idea, suggestion or thought is valid. Nothing is allowed to be ridiculed, criticized or corrected no matter how seemingly stupid or absurd. Outlaw comments such as, "That won't work." Sometimes the most ridiculous ideas trigger very good ones.

3. Discuss and write down topics and settings no matter how normal, strange or mundane. Divide paper in half. Label one column "Topic," and the other column "Setting." List *all* ideas. For instance, a topic could be "faith" and a setting could be "an elevator." It might not seem like much until you put two guys in an elevator talking about the importance of faith—and then the elevator breaks down. Other topics could be peer pressure, the meaning of love, jealousy, pettiness, hope, heartbreak, etc. Other settings could be a bus stop or station, park bench, living room, seats at a baseball game, church hallway, etc. Mix and match the topics and settings. Again, nothing is too outrageous (until you try to leave the room with it).

A hint about topics: Stick with universally applicable topics, not doctrinal issues, "gray areas," personal conflicts or private jokes. Rely mostly on exploring attitudes. For example, a script dealing with parent-child relationships may be better than a script dealing with the appropriate age or time to be baptized. (Reread the earlier part of this chapter on what to look for in a script for more explanation.)

4. Consider what kinds of characters you want. What type of people would be appropriate to play out the topics in those particular settings. Have your group members act out (improvise) some of the topics and settings. Let a couple of them (mixing and matching genders, too) act out different types of characters: a jock, nerd, gossipy busybody, tired homemaker, anxious teenager, domineering father, etc. See what you come up with. But don't get lazy. It's easiest to rely on stereotypical characters while the greater challenge is to come up with unique, true-to-life characters.

5. Develop a "hook" or a punch line at the end of the script. Particularly in comedy (but applicable to drama), many scripts work best with a "hook" or a punch line at the end. Sometimes an element of irony, contradiction, or silly twist can cause one character (along with the audience) to look bemused or chagrined.

One example of this is found in "The Sit-In" (see page 130). In this sketch, a young man presents a list of demands to his pastor. He threatens that if the demands aren't met, a "sit-in" will ensue in front of the church. After extensive negotiating, the pastor tries to diffuse the situation, but to no avail. Only at the end of the sketch do we find out that the young man is the pastor's son. (Sorry if we spoiled it for you, but it made a good example.)

Or there is a very popular Jeremiah People sketch that presents two gossipy women sitting on a back pew in a church with a little boy between them. The two women spend the entire sketch verbally destroying a number of people while the child takes it all in. At the end, when the child begins to imitate their attitudes, they are affronted and rebuke him sharply. "Where did he learn to talk like that?" one asks.

A good hook can turn a metal sketch to gold. So, go ahead. See what you can come up with. We dare you.

6. When all else fails—improvise. Improvise even if all else doesn't fail. For some tips and exercises about improvisation, take a look at the end of Chapter 5.

Getting It on Paper

At some stage past the brainstorming, improvisation and goofing off, somebody has to put something on paper. In other words, one lucky person gets to write the sketch or play. Whether it's handwritten, typed or word-processed, your cast needs those magical pieces of creativity in their hands.

Who gets the honor of writing the script? Probably the person who was foolish enough to go to the bathroom when the vote was taken.

This is a prime opportunity to enlist the help of that member of your congregation who has always enjoyed writing or might be studying English or journalism in school. It's surprising the number of potential writers who are hidden in the woodwork. Now is the time to seek them out and get them involved.

A little earlier we mentioned what to look for and what to avoid while script-hunting. The guidelines we gave apply equally to your own work. No exceptions or excuses.

Meanwhile, be a sensitive editor (and not only you but your whole group). Be objective. Imagine you are the audience. Think clearly about what parts you should keep and what you should throw out. A bit that seemed outrageously funny in the brainstorming session might really be merely a chuckle. Your favorite line in the entire script might need to come out. Be prepared for that possibility. Nothing you've done is sacred.

And when you've finished the editing, ask yourself: "Why would anyone care to see what we've put together? What's the point?" If you can positively answer those questions, then you've created a good script.

Incorporating Music Into Non-Musical Productions

Like everything else, music depends on your talent and resources. You can perform a straight play without any music at all, or you can do a variety show with songs that complement the mood and messages of several short sketches, or you can put together incidental music (piano or synthesizer) to lead into a sketch or indicate that a sketch has ended. And then there's always the popular "musical revue" approach that centers both sketches and songs around a specific theme. Music is also quite handy as a "cover" for set changes. Whether you use a piano, live band or tapes, music can help make set-change time go more quickly for your audience.

But What About Musicals?

Beware. Putting together a musical presents a whole new set of problems that you won't encounter in non-musical drama and comedy. The addition of music, songs and choreography will increase the demands on your group and the chances of things going wrong. Think of the work to find the right musical, then the production fees, then the sets, then the unique rehearsal schedules and problems, choreography, solo and chorus selections, rehearsals, costumes, orchestras, and the list goes on and on.

The question remains: Are you ready to do a musical? Do you have the resources and, especially, the musical expertise to make it work?

We're not trying to discourage you but—and it's a big one—a good musical is not the same as the Easter and Christmas cantatas your church has been doing since the beginning of time. It's a fairly ambitious undertaking. (Remember to have realistic expectations. Start small. Don't try to do too much. Brush after every meal. And don't forget all the other things we've been gabbing about for the last thousand pages.)

If you're ready—if you're *really* ready—then go ahead. And may God be with you.

4
Directing

("But I'm Not a Director!
How Can I Do It?")

Maybe you think you're not a director. We won't argue
with you. But somebody has to get the show going and
since you're the one reading this book, we'll assume that you got
stuck with the job. Tag. You're it.

Or maybe you want to direct. Maybe you know you don't have
the education or experience but you have a heart for it. Good for
you. That's as much as you'll need . . . for now. Know this: It is
possible to direct a production (whether it is a short sketch or a
longer play), but it ain't gonna be easy.

As director, there are a number of things that fall upon your
shoulders:

● You have to figure out what the sketch or play is about and
then guide your group into a clear representation of it on stage.

● You have to visualize the setting when no sets are available.

● Before a single person shows up for auditions you have to
see the characters come to life—how and where they move, how
they look, how they speak, how they think and why they think
that way.

● You have to be the eyes of the audience before the audience sees anything.

If the playwright is the composer of a theatrical symphony, then you, as director, are its arranger and conductor. (A rather poetic thought, isn't it?)

Okay, okay, so maybe we said too much too soon, and now you're wondering how you can be all those things when you barely even have time to read this book. We'll discuss each aspect of directing a little bit more.

The Director as Reader

As we've said already, read a variety of sketches and plays, and check out a few concise texts on directing. (We say concise because there are a lot of texts that scrutinize directing to the point of exhaustion.) Reading the texts won't hurt you. Honest.

Assuming the material you want to perform has been selected (if not, go back one chapter), you need to sit down and read it thoroughly—not as an interested party but as director. Read it once for your overall thoughts and reactions. Then read it again for a more critical analysis. Pinpoint your perceptions about story and plot. Think of who the characters are—their lives, feelings and personalities. Consider the language, mood and idea of the overall script. Know it as well as you can; you two are going to have to be friends for a few weeks.

As you read, ask yourself what type of material you're dealing with. Is it a comedy? drama? tragedy? melodrama? How does the material appeal to the emotions? the intellect? How will it ultimately appeal to the eyes? What do you visualize in your mind as you read it?

The Director as Observer

As director, you need to be an observer in several different ways. One way, and a fundamental rule to follow, is to attend some theatrical productions. And we're not referring *only* to your local community theatre group or high school drama department (whose productions you attend with a prayer that what you're about to see is worth two hours of your time). Your prayer might not be answered. Local productions are often good and they need your support, but the benefits that can be gained from experiencing live, professional theatre won't be equaled. Professional theatre is entertaining and educational. It gives you the chance to watch what other directors are doing with plays—sets, characters, line delivery, stage movement, etc. Think of how other directors make use of their money. What do they focus on? How can you adapt some of their ideas? Often such exposure will trigger your own creative juices for your particular production.

Another way to observe is to see some quality movies. (All film-burning denominations please move to the next paragraph.) However, seeing a good movie does not mean perusing a Christian film catalog or scanning your newspaper for that rarest of rare occurrences: a G-rated movie. Though you may be fortunate to find a good movie in one of those categories, the odds are not high. Try reading newspaper reviews or ask trustworthy (and obviously less spiritual) friends to recommend some movies of quality in content and execution. In case you don't have a newspaper or any friends . . .

Another form of observance is to go to a mall, bus station, airport—any place where people abound—and just watch them. (This is an exercise we'll suggest later for your actors.) Watch how people move, talk and interact. What actions are unique? What behavior is typical? Apart from being downright interesting, you'll pick up some valuable ideas for your production.

More specific to your role as director will be the necessity of observing your production as a member of the audience would. You, very literally, are the eyes of the audience before they ever see anything. Apart from your own feelings and goals for the play, you must anticipate what the audience will be feeling, and how you can help direct those feelings to a desired end. It's an important duality. You must have the subjectivity to work from a heart for the material, while maintaining the objectivity of those who will see it on stage for the first time. We've said it before, we'll say it again: Remember the needs of your audience.

The Director as Diplomat

Since the primary objective of this book is to deal with Christian productions, there are a few things beyond just directing that you'll need to consider:

1. Remember the age-old, ongoing battle for credibility. You'll have to show yourself credible for the church leaders and then show yourself credible to your cast and crew. Since you're directing, your cast will have to believe that you won't let them get up on stage and make fools of themselves—that your ideas really will work in front of an audience. Your crew will have to believe that doing those lights a certain way or having the spotlight come on at that time is truly a wise decision. Put yourself in their shoes (figuratively speaking), and be sensitive to their skepticism.

2. Realize your cast and crew might not be as dedicated as you are. Chances are, they won't be. But don't become a martyr. ("All right, go ahead and play in the church softball game instead of rehearsal. I'll rehearse around you . . . somehow." Deep, guilt-inducing sigh or self-righteous, "If I can put my time into it, then you can, too!") Remember, unless you're in a paid situation, most of the people are giving up their time to be a part of the production. Every now and again, they'll wonder why they're bothering (just like you will). You'll have to be the one to keep them together. You'll have to help them see the ultimate purpose (the scheme of eternity and all that, remember?). And more than likely, you'll have to be the one to make up for their lack of commitment. Be patient and don't be too hard on them. Even the disciples slept in the Garden of Gethsemane.

3. Head off the problem of ego and pride—yours and theirs. The best rule for combating this is the predetermined viewpoint that *you and your cast will do whatever is necessary for the good of the production.* Period. World without end. Amen. That means swallowing your pride in order to listen with an open mind to differing viewpoints, massage bruised egos, offer an apology even when you're not sure it was your fault, and tell the cast that they're doing a good job even if you don't feel like it anymore. But it also means asserting your authority when you have to, making decisions in spite of the "politics" involved, and often being perceived as "the bad guy."

Whatever is necessary for the good of the production. Make it your motto. But don't get a big head about it. Be on guard of your attitude—regardless of anyone else's. The quest for and achievement of power, on any level, can be corrupting. As director, it would be easy to simply try to make everyone do what you want them to do. Good luck. You might get away with it this time but not again. Volunteers don't take kindly to slave labor (even in the church). One thing "necessary for the good of the production" is that you keep your humility intact.

4. Treat the entire cast and crew as if they were the

main actors. Obviously, most of your time and attention will need to go to your leading actors, but it is important to balance that with time and attention spent on the rest of the cast and crew. Give love and attention to everyone as equals. Also, help the cast and crew members treat each other as equals. Build this sense of community, care and respect into your group by:

• beginning each rehearsal with prayer.

• preparing a Bible study on 1 Corinthians 12:12, "For just as the body is one and has many members, and all the members of the body, though many, are one body, so it is with Christ." Discuss what it means to be a part of one body and how all parts are important.

• assigning kids prayer partners. Have them pray for each other throughout the production.

• encouraging kids (and yourself) to look beyond the task at hand to their relationships with each other.

The Director as Picture-Maker

What the audience will ultimately see on stage is a series of living pictures. As director, you are the picture-maker. It's your responsibility to make the actors move around, on and off the stage, in a manner that will enhance the play. It's your job to make the actors seen and heard when they need to be and to keep the audience from being confused.

This function of moving the actors around is called blocking. (Don't ask us why. It probably comes from some root Latin word "blockus" later incorporated in football. Or maybe it comes from the idea that the stage is divided up into several "blocks"—bringing us to a dandy place for an illustration.)

Take a good look at Illustration 1. That's your stage as seen in terms of blocking. Here are your areas: up right, up right center, up center, up left center, up left, right, right center, center, left center, left, down right, down right center, down center, down left center, down left . . . hike!

"Whoa, now. Wait a minute. You mean the actors don't just climb up there and know where to go?"

Nope. The script will give you some help, but more will have to be added by you.

"Why? Why not let the cast do it?"

For one thing, your cast can't see themselves as you can from the audience. They might think where they're standing or how

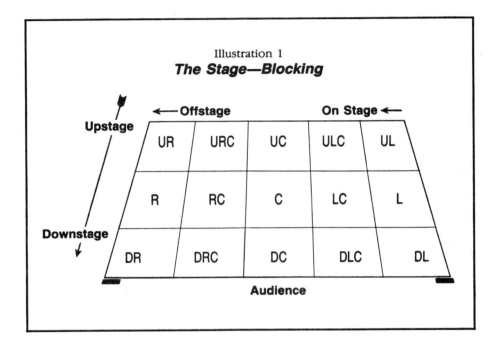

Illustration 1
The Stage—Blocking

they're moving looks all right. But it could be all wrong for the total picture from the audience. Maybe, from an audience perspective, the actors can't be seen well or heard clearly. It's your job to see that they are. You're going to turn the play into a series of pictures that will look and sound good. Blocking is the way to do it. And here's your basic vocabulary:

Stage right and *left* are from the character's viewpoint while on the stage looking at the audience (not the other way around).

Downstage is, obviously, down toward the audience. *Upstage* is farther away. Thus, having a character "move down" or "move up" is simply that—moving closer to or away from the audience. We're sure the terms come from original Greek words or Egyptian wall paintings (hieroglyphics, actually, but we didn't know how to spell it). To appease the purists who are still reading this text, the "up" and "down" refer to stages which, during Shakespeare's day, were sloped from high in the back to low toward the audience. This was a very utilitarian way of improving sightlines for the audience.

Offstage takes your characters away from the center of the stage, while *on stage* moves them closer to the center.

Easy, huh?

Since most of us are more attuned to television or movies rather than theatre, we're used to the camera directing our eyes. It's easy, then, to forget that there must be a center of attention on the stage or *emphasis* as someone called it. Without proper emphasis, the audience could become easily confused about where they should be looking. What character or area of the stage should command their attention at each specific moment? To create a proper picture for your audience, you must think of that question at all times.

Part of achieving this can be found in your actor's body positions on stage. Peruse yet another illustration (Illustration 2) and you'll see the various positions and their respective terminologies.

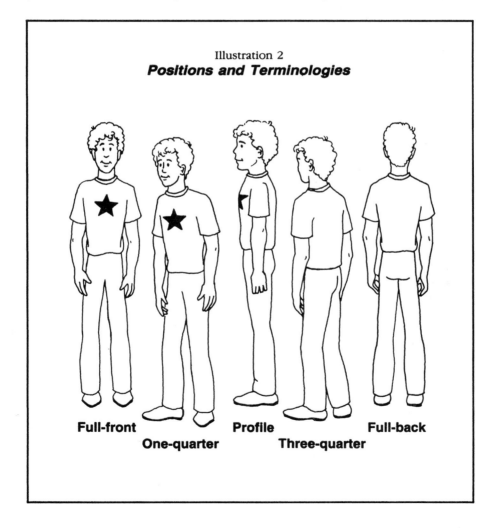

Illustration 2
Positions and Terminologies

Full-front   **Profile**   **Full-back**

One-quarter   **Three-quarter**

We have it from several good sources that the positions from strongest to weakest for your audience are full-front, one-quarter, profile, three-quarter and, as we already pointed out, full-back. In fact, the full-back is more than just weak, it's almost a sin. Drill into your actors that *they shalt not put their backs to the audience especially whilst delivering a line.*

Another thing to consider is that standing or sitting (not at the same time) is generally stronger than kneeling or lying down. Also, the position of the head will greatly affect the strength or weakness of body positions; for example, a stronger position for the head is level and facing toward the audience.

With two actors on stage, your picture becomes more complicated and their positions become increasingly important. Illustration 3 demonstrates different positions of two actors.

According to Webster, *upstaging* is "drawing the attention of the audience away from (a fellow actor) and to oneself by moving upstage so that the other actor must face away from the audience." Upstaging, as a practical rule, isn't a good idea

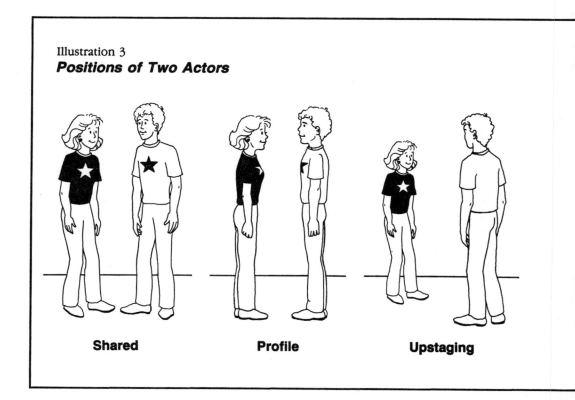

Illustration 3
Positions of Two Actors

Shared   **Profile**   **Upstaging**

but can be done through *cheating*—in which the downstage actor brings his or her body close to a profile position with head turned a little more toward the audience. Unless you're working with experienced people, we recommend that you stick with fundamental blocking. Leave the avant-garde stuff to other denominations for now.

And what if you have more than two people on stage at the same time? Then let them help you establish where the emphasis should be. Place them in such a way that the audience isn't looking over the entire stage trying to find out who they should be watching.

This can be accomplished several different ways. One way is through lines created by the bodies of the actors across the stage—straight, curved, diagonal or broken up. A second way is the popular triangle where two of the actors are positioned toward the audience with a third positioned farther away from the audience in the center. A third way is to place the actors around the stage so their focus of attention must be on the

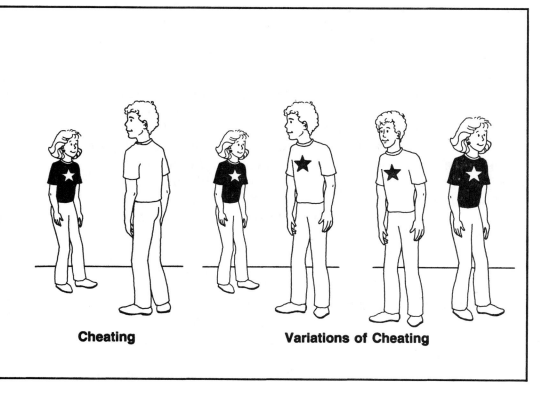

Cheating   **Variations of Cheating**

primary character. (For example, place the main speaker center or down right, and have the other actors face him or her down left.) A fourth way is to use your common sense. Look at the scene and notice where your eyes go naturally.

And that's actually a nifty little point for the entire process of blocking: Make sure that it is practical. Can your actors be seen? Can they be heard? Do they look natural and comfortable? That is the essence of making pictures for your audience.

The Director as Mover

Okay, fine. You've made a bunch of pretty pictures, but your actors aren't going to just stand still for the length of your production—no matter how much you might want them to, if only to keep them from bumping into each other. No, sirree, those folks gotta go somewhere or the cast and audience will slip off into Na-Na Land.

Some of the stage movements will be obvious from the script. It'll tell you where the characters should move and it'll be fairly clear why.

Other stage movements will be implied in the script. It might not say so directly, but you know the only way Aunt Matilda is going to give little Johnny that drink is for her to walk over and give it to him. (Unless, of course, Aunt Matilda is in a wheelchair and the miraculous healing scene isn't until later.)

Some stage movements won't be stated or implied but will be born out of necessity for practical or technical reasons—to get the actors where they need to be for a line or scene, to allow them to be seen and heard, to keep them out of the way of entering or exiting actors, to heighten comedy, to heighten the drama and emotion, to supplement dialogue, to keep your picture in order.

Though these situations will require creativity on your part, your imagination really gets to work in the non-specified movements. Most scripts will need you to add movement that will complement or enhance the story, mood and characters. Ask yourself where the scene is taking place and what would be the normal activity there. What is the emotional focus of the scene and how would the characters move in it? (For example, a funeral would have to be handled differently from an office party.) If a scene contains a lot of dialogue, would some movement help break up the potential monotony?

But before you have your actors bouncing off of the ceiling in frenzied activity, there are a few things you should know about stage movement:

1. A moving character will attract attention away from the character standing still. Therefore, actors should only move on their own lines and there should be purpose behind the movement—to give emphasis to the character or line, to draw the audience away from another part of the stage for some reason (to allow Bill the time to pull out a gun while we watch Bart go to the desk, etc.), or to draw attention to another part of the stage (because we know from an earlier scene that Bill has a gun in that desk and Bart doesn't suspect a thing).

2. If the character speaking is to cross another character, it should always be downstage from him or her.

3. Don't let your actors make the normal mistake of moving in a way that puts their backs to the audience or their faces away from the audience. It's easy to forget good body positions when moving. *Watch them closely*.

4. Movement can be critical to establishing or amplifying emotion; showing changes in characters or relationships; altering the direction of mood, dialogue or thought in a scene; revealing character; or setting up a line.

With all of that in mind, you must ask yourself who should be moving, what kind of moving should they do, when should they move, where should they move to, why are they moving at all, and how should they move?

5. Movement should break up potential monotony—thus, it should have enough variety to keep from becoming monotonous itself.

A Final Word

We encourage you to look through the resource section for other books to read that go into more depth and detail about directing. The more you read, the better you'll be as a director.

5
Acting Tips

*(Exercising Your
Acting Muscles)*

Acting is a very peculiar disease with equally peculiar contradictions. And folks in church represent them all. You'll find those who "live for acting" but couldn't act to "save their lives." You'll find others who wouldn't imagine trying to act, yet they perform extremely well on stage. There are those who will insist that they can't act and guess what? They're absolutely right. They can't. The list goes on and on. You'll get to meet all of these people eventually. Drama and comedy seem to attract a lot of the wrong people and exclude those who are best suited for it. (Sigh.) Such is life.

But this chapter is for *anyone* who is going to take a risk by climbing up on the stage. Because, when all the planning, directing, rehearsing, sweating, time and effort are done, "up on the stage" is where the production will succeed or not. Upon the actor falls the burden of bringing the character to believability—to life—while accurately representing the author's intent and the director's interpretation. The actor gets both the joy and frustration of being creative and imaginative but within the confines of the play's requirements.

Actors have to try to get the audience to respond even if the audience doesn't want to. You have to win them. Sometimes you'll make it and sometimes you won't. But at least you'll know you've done your best. This chapter will give you some help in acting to the best of your abilities.

Speech! Speech!

Unless you're pantomiming, all the great acting in the world won't mean much if you can't be heard or understood. Poor pronunciation (depending on characterization), mumbling, slurring, talking too fast, talking too slow, talking too soft (or the fear of being too loud), unintentional heavy accents, and other similar problems can destroy a production. This seems to be especially true for youth groups since many of the kids lack experience in acting or speaking in front of people.

The first thing that most beginning actors don't learn is how to use the diaphragm correctly, with deep and controlled breathing to get all of the way to the end of the sentence they are saying. (Go ahead, try that sentence and see how you do.) Such control is the essence of *projection* which will make all the difference in helping back-row listeners hear the lines, and preventing actors from becoming hoarse. The power behind the voice must originate in your breathing, not in your throat. The power behind the voice involves inhaling more actively than in normal speech and exhaling with more controlled pressure.

A second problem with most beginning actors is lack of *articulation*—using the mouth, tongue and teeth to say the words properly and clearly. Articulation involves relaxing the jaw, opening the mouth wide, and moving the tongue and lips to produce distinct sounds. Most beginners are afraid to do this because it feels funny. Most of us don't move our mouths that wide or speak so clearly in normal conversation. But stage is not normal conversation and, to be heard, good articulation must be achieved. If it's a real problem, remember one thing: It might feel funny but it won't look funny to the audience, it'll look quite natural.

Here are a few exercises to help with speech. Since projection and articulation involve overall physical relaxation, the first three exercises help you do that. The last two are designed to specifically exercise the voice:

● Achieve physical relaxation through tightening the body muscles. Make them as tense as possible, then relax them suddenly. Work from the tips of your toes to the top of your head, alternately tightening and relaxing muscles.

● Bounce around completely limp. Let your arms and head move freely and loosely.

● Slowly roll your head around in a complete circle, first clockwise then counterclockwise.

● Yawn. As long, deeply and loudly as possible.

● Exhale deeply and loudly through your vocal cords.

Once More With Feeling

If the director is responsible for guiding the production into a powerful representation of the play or sketch, then it is the actor's responsibility to ultimately "make it work" emotionally for the audience.

The interpretation of the character's lines by the director and actor helps clarify the lines' meaning, enhance the character, express the lines' emotional intent while leading to climax, and lend variety to the play.

Making sure the audience is really understanding the meaning and feeling of the lines can be achieved by some very obvious means. (The means are obvious, not because we think about them much, but because we don't think about them. When explained, you'll see how much a part of everyday use they are.) Ready or not, here they are:

1. There are four basic elements to using your voice: pitch, volume, tempo and quality. Pitch is the highness or lowness of sound, volume is the loudness, tempo is the rate, and quality is the timbre that distinguishes one voice from another. Each of these four elements can be used to your advantage for interpreting lines. Changing any one of these elements can heighten or diminish emotion. For example, a higher pitch can show high emotion and excitement, while a lower pitch can create the sound of authority, deep emotion, depression or anything Shakespearean (just kidding). The same is true for increases or decreases in volume or tempo. Practice talking fast and loud in front of the mirror and see if someone doesn't call the police.

2. Emphasis. Sometimes a word. Sometimes an entire line. Consider the question "What's that on the road ahead?" Say it. Now say it this way: "What's that on the road, a *head* ?" What's the difference? The difference is which word or words are emphasized in the line. Every line has one or two words that must be emphasized to say the line correctly. Most scripts will indicate by underlining or italicizing key words. Other times, key words are implied. If not, it's up to the director and actor to understand the character and scene well enough to know what's appropriate. Ask yourself how a line sounds if different words are emphasized. What sounds correct?

You can draw attention to a particular word or line or take away from its importance through emphasis or lack of emphasis—through a rise or fall in pitch, change in volume or tempo, or a pause right before a word or line is delivered.

3. Inflection—a change in pitch in the word being said. A voice can rise at the end of a word, fall at the end, or do both within the word. This can be a big problem for beginners since we're inclined to act the same way we read. For some reason we end each sentence or question with the same inflection, no variety. Watch it. It'll drive at least one person in your audience to extreme violence (two people if *we're* in attendance). And beware of how you interpret punctuation. A period doesn't mean your inflection always drops any more than a question mark means it must rise. Consider the thought, emotion, and speech patterns of the character within the scene you're playing.

4. Pause. This one is a toughie since most beginners (in church especially) are more interested in saying their lines and getting off the stage rather than taking the time for good, effective pauses. Fear of silence destroys one of the most effective tools you have for powerful communication. The pause, when handled properly, can be equally as powerful as any line delivered. A pause speaks volumes as long as it is justified and consistent with the character.

5. Rhythm. This is determined by the spacing between words, the frequency in delivery, how pauses are used, the emotional direction of the line and, as much as anything, whatever sounds natural and appropriate.

6. Responding. To put it simply, be a good listener. This not only applies to your lines but to how you respond to another character's lines. Don't just wait for him or her to finish a line so you can say yours. Be attentive and perceptive to what other characters are saying and how they're saying it so you can discern how to deliver your line.

Amazing how common-sensical these elements are. We use them all the time in our normal behavior and conversations, yet we toss them aside as soon as we step on stage.

Beware of the "typical" approach in how you say your lines. We all fall into the trap of taking the standard route rather than the correct one. A line that calls for anger is too often delivered by shouting. That's easy. And it's a sure sign of inexperience. Any time you try merging a lack of acting experience with strong emotion on stage, you wind up with extreme emotion. An angry character is typically portrayed by shouting or snarling through gritted teeth. A crying character is often portrayed by hysterics and whining. A laugh that should have been a chuckle becomes an outburst. Beware the obvious. Rather than this typical approach to saying lines, look for something more refined, more subtle (unless the script calls for it specifically). In other words, use what we call the Lamaze Method of Acting: natural line delivery.

What a Character!

Effective characterization on stage will often allow for a myriad of interpretations, discussions, debates, and even estrangements between actor and director, actor and other actors, and actor and the playwright's lawyer. Regardless, your mission (as the actor) will be to figure out who your character is and how to properly represent him or her on stage. You have several sources for determining this: the script, the director, outside resources and your own imagination.

From the script, you should determine these questions:

● Why is your character in the play at all? How does he fit in with the overall story?

● Is the character genuine or a caricature? What does she want?

● What is the character's driving force? What does he do in the play? What kinds of action does he take?

● What does the character say about herself?

● What do the other characters say about him? How does he relate to others? Who are his friends? enemies?

● What does the character look like? How old is she? How does she speak? walk? stand?

● What elements influenced the character by the time we see him in the play? What is his family background? religious background? economic background? emotional background? education? politics?

● What are the character's attitudes about different topics? What does she like? dislike?

● What kinds of adjectives would you use to describe him?

● What will the character become? Is she different at the end of the play than she was at the beginning? Why or why not?

● Write an imaginary biography about the character with as much detail as possible.

The director is another source for determining character qualities. You must be open to his or her interpretation and thoughts—like it or not. Unless you can argue something specific from the script itself, you must yield for the sake of harmony in your production. The director must have the final word. Listen attentively and discuss (not argue) various interpretations and which one will work best for you and the production (sometimes limitations will dictate what you can and can't do). But don't count on the director for every detail and nuance. Those are things only you as the actor can give.

An effective director will give you the time and enough of a creative rehearsal environment to experiment with your character.

Outside resources can be very informative about your character. A little research will go a long way if you can find and read articles, reviews and critiques of your play. Or if your play is based on some point in history, then research that period. Find out what was happening and why, and then try to understand how your character might fit into it. Sometimes there's a lot more information in background and history than even the playwright might have realized.

And then there's you. Somewhere in the combinations of chemicals that make you work, you're going to have to make the character real—first for you and then for your audience. If your character isn't believable to you, you'll have a difficult time convincing anyone else. Find the character within yourself by asking these questions: How much is the character like you? How are you different? Do you like the character? Why or why not?

An important key for discovering how to play the character is through observing. In your life, many things combine to give you insight and inspiration for your character: friends and acquaintances, strangers, everyday happenings, literature, movies, television, etc. Never portray a character through imitation.

Merely playing out a real person or another actor's rendition, a cliché or stereotype is cheating. Use your imagination. Take a little bit here and there to create something new and original for yourself. Let yourself go. You might surprise yourself with your new creation.

Acting

Earlier we called acting a disease of contradictions. Acting methods fit nicely into that category as well. If you want to learn about acting, there are a lot of people who'll go to their theatrical deaths claiming they have the better way for you to do it. Maybe some of the ways are great and helpful, but our advice is to take all we've already told you and just do it. Simple as that. Acting is the "ultimate pretend," a disciplined "make believe" that draws you and your audience into it. That's all.

Yes, there are plenty of extremes in acting exercises, if you want to try them . . . like dressing up as your character 24 hours a day and answering people only when they call you by your character's name (which can create a variety of problems, particularly if your name is Fred and your character's name is Trixie).

We've seen entire casts become completely neurotic about their production because they had just enough "method acting" to make them dangerous. They twisted, poked, probed and scrutinized their characters until they couldn't understand the character at all.

Our motto is: Good acting is good acting no matter how you get there. Just take what you can and do it. Think, imagine and experiment to develop your character. In rehearsals, concentrate on staying "in character," even if there are distractions or other actors fall out of character. As you get closer to the actual performance date, polish and refine your character. It'll grow as you grow. (Part of that is being prepared for rehearsals. You won't get the full benefit of them if you're trying to concentrate on that scene you should have already memorized while the director is trying to get you to concentrate on blocking. Do your homework.)

Whatever you do, be natural. If you're uncomfortable, your audience will be, too. If your performance is unrealistic or exaggerated (except for certain comic situations), your audience will dismiss your character as unbelievable. You're telling the audience that you don't really belong up there, you're just playing a part. The goal is to make them believe that you are the part. Even more simply stated: Being natural is an extension of being thoroughly in character, comfortable with your lines, and completely focused on your surroundings and how you fit into them. It's easy for some people. They seem to have an intuitive ability for getting on stage and making it look easy. For most people, though, it takes hard work and experience.

Comedy Versus Drama

There is an age-old battle in certain quarters about which is more difficult to do, comedy or drama? Both sides have excellent cases but we're inclined to say . . . both.

Drama and comedy are equally difficult. To do either with any effectiveness will always be a challenge and will require the interaction of all of the principles we've discussed so far. Good acting is good acting no matter what you're doing it in. (Sounds like a variation on another statement, doesn't it?) You might find comedy easier than drama, or vice versa—for you. Maybe you're more comfortable with comedy, or maybe you find drama more appealing, or maybe you find greater personal satisfaction in . . . well, you have the idea.

Memorizing Lines

Start memorizing as soon as you can. Don't wait for or rely on rehearsals to do it for you. There are several good ways to memorize:

● Go over the script page by page until you get it. Picture each page in your mind. As you remember specific lines, grasp the entire context.

● Put a sheet of paper on the page. Work your way down the page by keeping your lines covered (so you see the other character's lines but not your own).

● Go over your lines with other people in the play or with a friend who will read with you. It often helps to do this while walking. Don't focus on delivery—focus only on the words.

● Use a tape recorder. Record other characters' lines, and leave enough space for your lines. Then go over the script. One advantage to this technique is that you can actually rehearse while driving, if you have a cassette player in the car. The drawback is, of course, that you'll solicit a lot of stares from other motorists who see you talking to yourself.

● Highlight your lines with a highlighting pen or marker. This will help you visualize the script in your mind.

Calisthenics

There are some seemingly strange things you can do to "exercise" for acting. They're strange because you'll feel awfully silly if someone walks in on you while you're doing them. But they're fairly effective to stretch your acting muscles a little bit. (Thanks to Wendell Burton for some of these.)

1. Practice a variety of facial expressions in front of a mirror. (We said it before jokingly, but we're serious now.) Often the expression you think you're making isn't what you're really making. Look closely at what your face does when you're trying to frown, be sad, laugh or chuckle. Try a whole spectrum of emotions. Videotape your expressions. It's amazingly interesting to look at yourself!

2. Practice laughing by thinking of the funniest things you can: an incident, something you heard, a bit from a television show or movie. Practice making your laugh sound spontaneous and natural.

3. Practice crying by recalling something that makes you sad—real or imaginary. Concentrate on a distinct pain you remember experiencing. Recall how it felt and what it did to you emotionally and physically.

4. Imagine yourself in a particular location—your favorite place—from childhood. Close your eyes and imagine it all around you. Use your senses to recreate it in your mind. Imagine you are touching the things that surround you. Imagine the sounds that filled the place (or the silence), the smell and the taste (if any).

5. Imagine holding something in your hands that you treasured (and possibly lost) at least five years ago. See it in your mind. What did it look like? Concentrate on what it feels like to hold it again. What emotions do you feel?

6. Go to a bus station, mall, shopping center—anywhere with a lot of people—and simply observe. Watch how the people walk, interrelate and conduct themselves. Notice their facial expressions, voices and attitudes. Do you see anything interesting? Is there anyone or anything you can mimic? (We don't suggest you do it there, you might get hurt.)

7. Pretend you're a machine with moving parts (moving your arm up and down, your body back and forth, etc.). Begin moving one of those parts. Have others join in, one at a time, synchronizing their actions to yours. Eventually you'll create what appears to be a complete machine with coordinating moving parts in operation. This helps develop individual and group body control.

8. Choose an object in nature (tree, flower, etc.) and try to physically recreate its growth from when it was a seed.

9. Recreate a scene in your mind of something that has happened that day (going to the refrigerator, getting out milk, pouring it into a glass, etc.). Then act out that scene in slow motion. Are you able to keep a consistent speed? Does it look and feel real?

10. Observe, then mimic the actions of some of your favorite animals. (Please limit this to earthbound creatures. We don't want to be sued if someone decides to screech like an eagle and then jump off a building in the name of acting.)

Improvisation

Unlike acting exercises, improvisation is more focused in its structure. You or your actors take an imaginary situation or conflict and improvise (thus, the name) all of the lines and action. It ain't easy, but it is worthwhile for developing skills in character and believability. Here are some basic rules for improvisation:

● The best improvisation completely pantomimes objects or props.

● React *and* initiate conversation and action. Don't just wait until somebody else says or does something before you react.

● Allow minimal or no physical contact.

● Always have a starting point. Clearly explain the situation, then give a cue to begin.

● Don't worry about a specific ending. Give a set amount of time at the beginning of an improvisation, or simply end when it begins to drag.

● Keep the energy high at all times.

Now, here are a few situations for you to improvise. Remember to keep the energy up, and try to pantomime all objects and props. If things begin to drag, quickly insert someone else into the scene or stop it and start another. The director's or leader's role is critical here. Let's go:

1. Two people meet in a bargain basement. An imaginary table piled high with scarves sits in the center. A casual conversation ensues until both find a scarf they like. When they pull it out, they discover they are holding opposite ends of the same scarf. A "heated" discussion begins.

2. A jealous husband goes with his wife on her first driving lesson with a good-looking, but very innocent driving instructor.

3. Two people are watching television in the lounge area of a college dormitory. A third person enters and interrupts their viewing by trying to sell them something.

4. One person is the head of a exchange/refund department in a large department store. A number of people come by, one at a time, trying to return merchandise—both real and imaginary.

5. A young man with a sizeable opinion of himself takes a young lady out—a lady he wants to impress. The date is at a restaurant he thinks is the best but, to the girl, is a dumpy travel stop complete with obnoxious waitress.

6. A young couple is on their honeymoon at a beach. A conversation ensues and, as they talk, they are asked to switch emotions on cue while maintaining a reasonable amount of sense in the conversation. Emotions to use: giddy joy, distrust, worry, laughter, etc.

7. Pull a paragraph from a famous play or movie and have an individual read it normally. Then alter how it is read by having him or her do it in different styles: Shakespeare, soap opera, western, etc.

8. Have two people start a conversation while acting out the game "Twister." At an appropriate time, tell them to freeze. Replace one of the people with someone else who must assume the exact same physical position. When they "unfreeze," the new person must initiate and carry on the conversation—only on a completely different subject, justifying the odd physical position they are in since they are no longer playing "Twister." For example, the actors could pretend they are looking for a contact or a lost billfold. They continue with the conversation and think of some other physical activity such as dancing. They could say, "I feel so happy I found my contact, I feel like dancing." Freeze the actors during their dancing, then substitute new people who must justify their strange position. Continue in this manner until several people have had a chance to improvise.

9. A young man takes his fiancee out to dinner the night before the wedding to tell her he's not going through with it.

10. Noah is building the ark and his disgruntled wife comes out and asks him what he's doing. She complains that none of the chores are getting done around the house, etc.

11. A husband and wife with two young children are on their way to church to see a film about family unity. What happens in the car exposes their need for the message.

12. Six young people are in a van on the way to a ski retreat. The youth leader is driving and trying to start a discussion about what God has been doing in their lives lately, but the passengers are more interested in other things.

13. A person visits a psychiatrist because every time he coughs he starts to laugh uncontrollably—until he sneezes, then he instantly stops laughing. This can be expanded by having the person cry whenever the psychiatrist says the word "you" or snaps his or her fingers.

14. Two little children observe and make comments during their first time in the main worship service at church.

15. An old man and an old woman, both widowed a number of years ago, go on their first date and end up talking about marriage.

16. A young man (or woman) returns from Europe having been gone for over a year without telling anyone where he's been or what he was doing. He has come back to ask forgiveness from his father for running off. He arrives unannounced. His surprised sister (or brother) must tell him of his father's death and her own bitterness over the situation.

17. A shy 16-year-old girl is caught shoplifting. While being questioned, we discover she is actually from a wealthy family and why she stole the merchandise. (Or she could be the daughter of a pastor.)

18. Three people are trapped in a small, cold mine shaft. Realizing they are facing death, their conversation covers everything from a hopeful rescue to "black humor" to resolute despair.

19. A guy and girl are on their first date at a movie theatre. In his haste to make a good impression, he does everything wrong—from spilling popcorn on her lap to bumping her face as he tries to put his arm around her. (Be careful.)

20. Two girls are sitting on a park bench, each waiting to meet their date for the evening. In the process of their conversation, they discover—to their horror—they're both waiting for the same guy. (Make sure you find out about this guy in bits and pieces until the point of realization.)

6
Auditions

*(If All the World's
a Stage, Where Are
the Actors When
You Need Them?)*

If you want to form a drama and comedy group that will meet on a fairly regular basis, what is your ultimate aim? (Goals, remember?) Will you work toward a production? do workshops? sit in a circle and stare at each other? What will you do from meeting to meeting? What will you call the group? Will you limit membership to only youth group members? What are the specific age limitations, if any are needed?

A warning about putting together an acting group: We live in a task-oriented society. People want to see results. Most of your members will probably want to feel like they're working toward something. What will they work toward? Simply becoming better actors? Nah. The die-hards will go along with that, but most of your members will wonder if they aren't better off in the choir. (At least they are seen occasionally.) Chances are your church leaders will begin to wonder what your acting group is up to, also. Realize now that meeting for the sake of meeting won't last long.

For a production, you'll have to understand your characters

and, from that, decide whether you want to conduct auditions to fill the parts, choose the people yourself, or put names in a hat and draw them while blindfolded.

Let's break that last paragraph down a little bit and gab about each element.

Who Can Audition?

When you put together a specific production, you're going to need people to play the parts. But who will you get to fill the parts? Will you use only the people in your drama and comedy group? Will you include only youth group members and exclude others? Will you encourage sponsors and parents to audition? Will you open up auditions to the entire church?

When directing a specific, short-term production that calls for varied ages, try not to limit your cast by staying with people all the same age. Actively recruit and mix ages, if you can. If you have a script that calls for an older person, don't take the easy way out by filling the role with one of your youth group members. Ask an older person to play the role. Not only is it far more realistic but far more satisfying as well. Some of our best experiences have been with casts of mixed ages—watching them relate to each other, learn from each other and grow. It adds an element of life to a production that you won't get with casts all the same age.

Getting the Word Out

Once you've decided who you'll target for characters for a production, how will you let these people know about auditions for parts? Within the church, you have some clear resources: announcements in newsletters or worship bulletins; from the pulpit; in various classes; in youth group meetings; and the strongest communicative device, word of mouth.

You'll be surprised at who'll express an interest. Then again, maybe you won't.

You'll likely hear from those who have always acted, want to do it now, and always will do it. With great determination, they'll assail you with their theatrical viewpoint and will ultimately leave you an empty shell of the person you were when you started working with them. They'll carry on unscathed while you join the littered trail they've left behind of the corpses of other church leaders they've worked with.

You'll hear from those who fit into that stereotypical category of "theatre enthusiast." These people are creative enough to be interesting, but eccentric enough to be downright weird.

You'll hear from all kinds: those whose parents made them; those who've always wanted to act but didn't know where to start; those who never wanted to act but didn't want to sing in the choir; those who've always been stuck with the task because of good appearance or voice, and they feel obligated to audition; and on and on.

And you might not hear from anyone at all.

Be prepared for all of the above.

Remember, be organized before you advertise for auditions. Know your goals and objectives and develop a reasonable plan. If you are unorganized, you'll begin on a shaky foundation. Go back to Chapter 2 if you're still unsure about how to set goals.

Auditions: Getting Ready

Right. Auditions can be a pain in the petunias. It's easier to ask certain people you know would fit a role perfectly. But auditions give everyone a fair chance at the roles. In church, where such selection is taken more personally and less professionally, giving everyone a fair chance is critical. We advise you to remain objective and avoid casting in advance of auditions. To cast in advance (or be suspected of doing it) will make you shark bait for the rest of your natural life.

"Wait a minute. What if I don't want to open the production to everyone? What if I know George over there would be perfect for the part? What if I know Janet has always shown an instinctive ability for acting and should be a part of the cast?"

Sometimes, in the face of such clear choices, standard auditions *might* not be necessary. You can talk with the people individually for a "private audition," getting their feelings about the role and how they could be involved.

An advantage to this personal approach is that you get exactly who you want without the muss-and-fuss and ego-on-the-line problems of standard auditions. If you handpick, you'll get people who are more in line with your goals, the vision you have for the production, and your personality.

A disadvantage to this personal approach, besides the unfairness, is that you limit yourself, your characters and your group. The personal approach is too often the easy way out of stretching beyond your immediate circle of youth group members, friends and acquaintances. You take the chance of losing your open-mindedness to outsiders and objectivity about the direction of your group.

In other words, *be extremely careful* with this sort of casting.

But, hey, don't worry. Auditions can be a fairly simple process if you go into them with the right attitude and some preparation.

Prior to auditions you need to analyze your characters. What kind of personality do they have? What should they look like? What kind of voice do they have?

Select key portions of the script for your participants to read and act out. What sections will reveal the most about the character and the person auditioning for it? Consider different moods and demands the script makes on the actor.

Put together an audition form similar to Illustration 4. During the audition, distribute the forms and ask the participants to fill out the top portion. Leave room at the bottom of the form for you to write your thoughts about each person's audition.

Prior to auditions, you also have to consider what order you want to try out the various characters. We suggest you audition one character at a time: all the Aunt Sarahs, then all the Uncle Bills, then all the little Davies. Once you've done that, try mixing and matching those who've auditioned to see how they interact with each other. Watch how they look together physically—height, family resemblances, etc.

Now that you've thought through these preliminary questions, decide the audition's date, time and place. Announce the audition, then do it.

Auditions: Doing Them

At the beginning of an audition, make certain you do all you can to relax and encourage those auditioning. Begin with a prayer; lead a few warm-up exercises or improvisations (see Chapter 5); and maintain an upbeat and positive attitude.

The standard audition involves calling the name of the participant, putting him or her on stage to read the preselected scenes alone or with other participants, briefly explaining the scene, and writing your notes about his or her basic acting ability (How did he or she do? Will you need him or her for "call-backs"—meaning that you thought he or she was good, and you want him or her to read again). When the audition is

Illustration 4
Audition Sheet

Name _____Phone_____Date_____

Address _____
　　　　　Street　　　　　　　　　City　　　　State　　　Zip Code

Year in school___Age___M__F__Height___Weight___Hair color___

● Do you sing?____ If yes, what is your voice range? _____

● Do you play a musical instrument?____ If yes, what type of instrument? _____

● Do you dance?_____ If yes, what type of dance? _____
  _____

● When would you be able to rehearse? (Mark first, second and third
  choice.)

Monday evening	_____
Tuesday evening	_____
Wednesday evening	_____
Thursday evening	_____
Friday evening	_____
Saturday morning	_____
Saturday afternoon	_____
Saturday evening	_____
Sunday afternoon	_____
Sunday evening	_____

. . . . .Do not write below this line . . . .

Appearance:　　　　　　　Ability to take direction:

Voice:　　　　　　　　　　Sense of comedy:

Movement:　　　　　　　　Other:

Emotion:

Call back for role of: _____

over say in a non-committal, distant-yet-encouraging-and-kind tone, "Thank you. Next, please."

Okay, maybe we said that flippantly, but the truth is that you must remain objective throughout the audition. You can't betray to anyone that you've made some sort of mental decision until everyone has auditioned. You must also make it clear that many factors are involved. No one will automatically get a role if he or she read well or not get a role if he or she didn't read well. People's egos are involved so always be tactful, assuring and diplomatic.

Also, make sure all participants understand your anticipated rehearsal schedule and expectations. Explaining the schedule and expectations weeds out some people immediately.

Here are several questions you must consider as your actors are auditioning:

● Is there something about each person's personality that seems to match the character?

● What quality is her appearance, voice and speech?

● What kind of stage presence and poise does he have? Does he show strength or weakness?

● How much does she add to the character? Was the reading "functional"?

● How was his timing?

● Do you think the audience will like or dislike her? Will they sympathize with her or not care at all?

● Is he funny?

Be careful with readings. A person may read horribly the first time but excel once he or she is "warmed up." Others may read extremely well but never grow beyond that. Call-backs give you a second chance to hear people read, and it gives the actors a second chance to show what they can do with the part.

If you decide you want to call back a person, here are some things to look for. (Be sure to mix and match the characters, as we suggested before.)

● More details about the person's ability to portray the character.

● The person's ability to think quickly on stage and respond spontaneously. (You might try some improvisations to uncover this.)

● The person's interaction with other actors on stage.

● The person's ability to read. (Was the reading better or

worse than the first time?)

When the time comes for you to make final choices—and before you make any announcements—bring in the actors for a final reading to see how the entire group looks and sounds. At this point, present a more detailed explanation of your expectations and the actors' obligations in schedule and time.

Prior to assigning parts, consider whether you want to have understudies. (These are the people who play "standby" to your main actors in case something happens to keep them away from rehearsals or the actual performance.) If you select understudies for all of the main characters, you can often have them prepare for a second role. The problem with understudies is finding people who are willing to sacrifice time and energy for what may be a fruitless role.

In the slim chance that your church or youth group abounds with acting talents, double-casting is another option. You could assign roles for two casts. Cast A could perform a couple of nights, and Cast B could perform a couple of nights. Only you will know what casting options will work in your church.

What About Parents?

When you're dealing with children or teenagers, always keep the parents out of the audition area. Then the kids won't be distracted, you won't have to deal with the parents, and the other participants whose parents couldn't be there won't feel unfairly treated (since they didn't have the benefit of parental coaching and support).

Once you have completed auditions and chosen the actors, it's best to keep parents from attending the rehearsals. Occasionally, parents will push to get their kids the best parts or more attention; at other times parents may be overly critical of their kids' attempts at acting; still at other times parents may be critical of your attempts at directing. Avoid these potential problems by telling the parents your goals for the production. Emphasize that the purposes of your production are to give kids a chance to try something new, to develop their own creativity, to meet new friends and to stretch beyond themselves.

Parents may want to attend auditions and rehearsals simply because they want to help. Allow parents to help in other ways such as making telephone calls, sewing costumes or building sets. Affirm parents for their good intentions, but emphasize that the production is for their kids.

What About All Those Good-Hearted People Who Can't Act?

Every youth group and church have them—those people who are willing to do anything for your production. They always audition, but they never get the part. The reason is simple: Equal to their spirit of sacrifice is their seeming lack of talent. You've worked with them and you've worked with them, but to no avail. Unfortunately we can't advise you to put them on stage anyway, as much as you might want to. To do so would be counterproductive. We *can* advise you to remember that God has given everybody unique gifts. Try to find each person's gifts and use them. For example, maybe an individual can't sing or act, but he or she can print, draw and paint. Then use that person to create sets and design the program.

Behind-the-Scenes Decision-Making

For the sake of your production, you must privately ask yourself questions about the people who have auditioned—questions that go beyond what you saw on stage.

● Will the people really commit themselves? What is their "track record" for commitment to other church or youth group activities? Do they begin a project enthusiastically and then drop out in the middle?

● If they are committed, are they overcommitted? In other words, are they involved in so many things that they couldn't possibly do the best job in your production?

● Will they be conscientious?

● Will they cooperate and follow your direction?

● By virtue of their personality, will they add or distract from rehearsals?

● What is their temperament?

● Are their expectations of the production realistic? (They might expect even more than you do and get frustrated when you don't deliver.)

● Will you have a power struggle with them?

● How are their memorization skills?

● Are they consistent in their attendance at church and youth group or do you think they're joining just to "be in the spotlight"?

● What are the personal ramifications of choosing one person over another?

● How are the people perceived by your pastor? your church leadership?

● If you've auditioned young children for a specific production, are you also prepared to deal with their parents? (You must consider this. You won't have one without the other.)

Once you've made your decisions, know clearly in your mind why you've made them and be prepared to articulate those thoughts. You'll have to. (You'll see why in just a minute.)

Communicating the Decisions

One way to communicate decisions is to post the decisions in a prearranged and conspicuous place such as a church bulletin board, newsletter or Sunday bulletin.

Another way to communicate decisions is to send out letters with the announcements of who is assigned the parts. Include a thanks to everyone who auditioned.

Still another way is to make personal phone calls or face-to-face appointments. The drawback to this one, however, is that you put yourself in an uncomfortable position of answering "why Judith got the part and I didn't."

Avoid announcing role assignments in youth group meetings. The kids who didn't receive a part may feel devastated when they find out. This feeling is intensified when others are around and hear the decisions.

Your method of communicating decisions is up to you. Whatever you do, be kind and encouraging. Assure the participants that the decision was made for a variety of reasons, not necessarily because of a lack of acting talent or ability.

Living With Your Decisions

Once you've made your selections for the production, we suggest that you leave town, or if that isn't possible, disconnect the phone and hide in the basement for a few weeks.

Johnny might be a little hurt that he didn't get the part, but Johnny's parents might be inclined to change their membership to another church over the issue.

Words and phrases like "narrow-minded," "tyrant," "my cat could direct better than you," "precasting" and "it'll be a horrible show" will be sent your way. Count on it.

Know firmly why you made your choices and be prepared to respond if asked. Be gentle, civilized, and intelligent in your responses and you'll make it through with minimal physical damage.

What About the Rest of Them?

Apart from yourself and your actors, who will help you with behind-the-scenes work? You can't handle all of the details.

We heartily suggest that you ask someone with organizational skills to assist you. This person can create a list of members' names, addresses and phone numbers. He or she can help call members for meetings, rehearsals, or any of the other myriad of details that'll destroy your time if you have to do all the work. If you can't find an organized, detail-conscious person to help you, be prepared for a few late nights covering the details yourself. Organization is necessary to the effective functioning of your production. Otherwise, you'll be batting your head against the proverbial wall and your cast and crew will slowly desert you. Nobody likes to waste his or her time.

It's not easy to find people to build sets, make costumes, organize makeup, coordinate sound or lights—all the behind-the-scenes jobs necessary to get a show together. More than likely you and your cast will be involved in all aspects. But sound and lights? Whoops.

If your church has a department in charge of lights and sound, then go to those people and try to involve them in your production.

If not . . .

As you did with the actors, put out a plea to your congregation and youth group through the usual methods. As we mentioned before, you could involve some of the people who tried out for parts, but didn't get one. (Use only the people you know could do the job.) You could involve people with interests in these areas. Otherwise, you might have to ask specific people directly— whether they know much about each area or not.

If you can't find anyone in your church to handle behind-the-scenes work, look for people in other churches, or ask someone from the secular field. Involving someone who isn't active in church could be a potentially strong outreach, and it could have a tremendous impact on that individual.

Whomever you involve, ask yourself many of the same questions you asked the actors:

- Does he have a special talent that matches the job?
- Can she get along with others?
- Does he take suggestions willingly?

And smile. These are the trials that will help you grow.

Non-Auditions

For an ongoing drama and comedy group, you might not want to schedule a standard audition since your participants aren't necessarily reading for a specific part. You could announce a meeting and invite all interested people to bring a prepared monologue, sketch or selection from a well-known work.

During the initial meeting for interested individuals, you could ask the participants to try some improvisations and acting exercises. Here are a few exercises to help you clarify the abilities of those who have shown an interest in the group. (For other acting exercises, see Chapter 5.) Thanks again to Wendell Burton for some of these ideas.

1. Have the actors impersonate (accurately, not cruelly) someone they know from their past. Have the group ask the impersonators questions about who they are, what they do, how they know the person impersonating them, etc.

2. Cut out magazine pictures of interesting-looking people—no names—and distribute the pictures to the participants. One at a time, ask each actor to stand up and use his or her imagination to portray the person in the picture.

3. Think of a variety of situations—conflicts, confrontations, embarrassments, familiar play or movie scenes, personal experiences—and ask different members to act them out. For example, "You're on a date with a person you really want to impress. You're at a restaurant and eating spaghetti." Or, "One person is an extremely shy visitor to youth group. Another person must try to get the visitor to talk and participate in the activities."

4. Put everyone in a circle (or divide into twos or threes if your group is large) and, one at a time, ask the participants to talk to the person on their right as if they were someone else. (Someone not necessarily known by the group but from the participants' past or present who conjures up positive or negative emotions—a long lost friend, someone who hurt them, a teacher who helped them, etc.) The person being spoken to must do his or her best—without knowing who he or she is—to react, ask questions, and figure out what's going on. Yeah, it sounds like one of those "psycho group sessions" but it can be very insightful.

5. Distribute 3×5 cards and pencils. Ask everyone to write down one sentence on the card. The sentence could be anything from "How are you today?" to "The cow jumped over the moon." Mix the cards and hand two or three to a couple of your members. Ask them to create a scene from the sentences on the cards.

6. A commonly used exercise is "Fall Into the Circle." A group of six or eight people form a tight circle. A volunteer steps to the center of the circle, closes his or her eyes and allows himself or herself to fall stiff-legged backward. The people in the circle gently push the person back and forth to one another never allowing him or her to fall. Be very careful with this exercise. Make sure no one in the group thinks it would be funny to let the person fall. Also make sure everyone can physically handle catching the person. When done properly, this exercise can teach a lot about trust and relaxation.

7. Blindfold one person. Ask another individual to lead the "blind" one around the room or over an obstacle course. At various points, the blind person should be given objects to touch and describe. This can be a great deal of fun and heighten sensory perception.

8. Line up your group into four or more parallel lines. Everyone should be facing the same direction and standing arms-length apart with arms raised to shoulder level. Two volunteers begin slowly walking between the rows. The director loudly says "Streets" and the people in the lines do a quarter turn to their right, or "Avenues" in which they go back a quarter turn to the left—arms still extended. The two walking through the rows must change direction as the lines change. Apart from trying to get through the maze, this teaches both the couple and the people in the lines how to create a quick and coordinated response.

9. Divide into couples and have one person become a mirror. Every move the one person makes, the other person must copy. The individuals should be encouraged to do this at varied speeds and with varied size of movement.

10. Have everyone get into a crouched position. On the count of three, they should "explode" into another position and hold it. Slowly, almost imperceptibly, ask the participants to begin to change position into something else. This is a challenging exercise for body control and concentration.

Battling the Bureaucracy

Depending on the size of your church, you'll have to juggle your production or group against any number of different activities. Thoroughly check out church, youth group and school calendars. Take absolutely nothing for granted, or you'll show up one night for a rehearsal and you won't have a meeting place or half of your cast and crew because of some other activity.

Make sure your meeting place is suitable for an acting group. The room should be large and spacious enough for actors to move about freely during acting and improvisation exercises. If the room is too small or if you find yourself dodging tables every time you meet, you'll have trouble.

Be diplomatic with the person in charge of coordinating meeting times and places, but don't let yourself get pushed around just because you're the new activity in church. If you have too many difficulties in scheduling places and times, the quality of your group or production will suffer. Play by the rules but go to the highest authority if the rules keep working against you.

Well?

How do you feel now? A little tired? Maybe just a bit bug-eyed at the thought of all of this? Take heart. The fun is just beginning . . .

7
Production

*(The Fearful Journey Into
the Unknown—or,
Lighting, Sound, Props,
Costumes, Makeup,
Promotion and Other
Things Determined to
Ruin Your Show)*

Creating big, bombastic, overblown mega-productions is not our focus for this book. They have their places (as do root canals, British sitcoms and CB radios), but few churches have the money, time, talent, resources and energy necessary for mega-productions.

This chapter will help you do what is necessary to put on a program just right for your church or youth group. We subscribe to three basic principles of production: KISS, KICC and KIMM.

1. The KISS principle: Keep It Simple, Stupid. A charming and endearing phrase it's not. But it can't be overstated. Simplicity is one of the first keys to success in many amateur (and professional) productions. Oftentimes, more can be accomplished with two folding chairs and two actors than with a detailed set complete with backdrop, smoke machines, live animals and a cast of hundreds. Poor production draws attention to itself and away from the theme. Balance, remember?

2. The KICC principle: Keep It Clean, Camel-breath. This principle ranks right along with the first one—not very endearing, but valuable to remember. Little things like tidiness on stage are parts of what separate totally amateur productions from first-rate productions. This principle is particularly true in a fast-paced, short-sketch format, where chairs and props are moved and removed rapidly. After each segment, the stage should look clean and neat, as if you were just starting the production.

3. The KIMM principle: Keep It Moving, Meathead. More verbal abuse to remind you that production pacing is critical. This principle does not refer to the actors' pacing or their line delivery but to those moments between scenes or sketches where bodies, props and set pieces are being moved. This must be done quickly, quietly and efficiently. It is surprising (at least it is to most people) how a production can be well-conceived, well-written and well-acted, but come to a grinding halt with poor production pacing.

This principle is best accomplished by assigning a small stage crew expressly to reset the stage. Or in the case of small productions, the cast should be given production tasks such as removing chairs, adjusting microphones or handling props. These assignments should be rehearsed as diligently as any acting scene. And believe us, the payoff will be obvious both in program length and flow.

We'll mention again that simple music covers set changes and gives the audience something to listen to during the short time between scenes or sketches.

The whole premise of quality, particularly in thematic Christian productions, is to enhance the focus of the script. Let's talk about some key elements of a good production.

Props: A Treatise on Canes and Costumes

Props (short for properties) are items which bring realism to the stage and help transport the audience to the time or location where the action occurs. These include set props (large items like furniture, rugs, drapes, trees, rocks, etc.); trim props (small items added to decorate); and hand props (smaller items often carried or used by the actors themselves).

Props exist to enhance and enrich a performance, not to become crutches for the actors. Too often, amateur productions and actors rely on props to shore up their weaknesses. But a crutch, no matter what shape, color or degree of beauty, is still a crutch and will glaringly draw attention to itself.

A classic example of using a prop as a crutch is the young actor who always uses a cane when portraying an elderly person. Of all the elderly people you know, how many use a cane? Not as many as our "stage" elderly, that's for sure. Yet we allow ourselves to be convinced that this prop will strengthen our character portrayal. On the contrary, the audience will probably be more likely to notice the cane than to believe this actor truly is old.

How can you help your actors "be" their characters and not rely on props? How do you help them portray characters realistically? Easy. Send the actors to Chapter 5 and tell them to *observe real people*. Does a cane make people old? No. Their posture, the length and rhythm of their step, their clothing, pronunciation and numerous unique actions make people who they are. A cane in the hand of the actor no more makes him or her old than a piano in your garage makes you a pianist. (Gosh, what a beautiful and weathered illustration.)

Always ask: Is this prop necessary? If the answer is no, continue to develop the characters and make them believable without the use of props. If the answer is yes, look for just about any prop (barring the very unusual) in your local Salvation Army, Goodwill or thrift store. Even most of the smallest of towns have some type of thrift outlet where used items may be purchased. If you've never ventured into a thrift store, try it. The fun you'll have exploring is worth the trip.

These stores are also great places to find many of the costumes you'll need. Make your costumes as realistic as possible so your characters will be believable. Beware of stereotypes. Not all grandmothers wear shawls, not all little boys wear shorts and suspenders, not all little girls wear ribbons and ruffles, not all ill people wear hospital gowns, not all athletes wear warm-up suits.

Be creative as you choose an appropriate costume. The best way to do this is to observe (once again). Look at people who are similar to the characters in your production. Glance through magazines and books, watch movies or television. When you find ideas, write them down. From these ideas, create a costume that is right for your character.

If you decide you need a detailed, specialized costume, you could buy it at most costume companies. (A list of costume companies is included in the resource section.) Most of these companies offer complete catalogs upon request. However, don't overlook the possibility of having the actors search their closets for necessary items. Or distribute a "costumes-needed" list to the congregation; see what some of the members will donate or loan. You also may find that a good seamstress is quietly hiding somewhere in your church or organization. Always look internally first to fulfill your production needs. Do this not just to cut financial corners, but to involve people in what will prove to be a meaningful and fun experience. It's amazing the number of people—beyond the same old seven who do everything—who are simply waiting to be asked.

Here are some questions to consider when acquiring props and costumes:

1. To make our production the best it can be, what set props will we need, if any? rugs? sofas? drapes? backdrops?

2. If we need backdrops to represent certain scenes, who will make them? What materials are necessary? boards? paint? brushes? Can we recruit carpenters from church to help? Can we use people who didn't receive an acting part, but who are skilled in painting and design? (More on sets construction later in this chapter.)

3. Where can we get the set props? Should we put out a request to the congregation? Do the actors have pieces we could borrow?

4. What trim props will we need? pictures? lamps? Where can we get them? from the actors? congregation? Salvation Army? Goodwill?

5. What hand props are needed? books? pots and pans? flashlights?

6. What costumes would be the most believable for each character? Who will need eyeglasses? hats? coats? pants? dresses? purses? What type of shoes?

7. Will each person need more than one change of costume for the production? If so, what changes are necessary? Can the changes be done simply and quickly?

8. Where can we get the costumes? at home? from friends? church members? thrift stores?

9. Do we have a budget for props and costumes? If so, what can we afford?

10. Will the costumes and props enrich and enhance the production? If they won't add quality to your production and characters, don't use them.

Kiss and Makeup

In the words of the robot from that now-classic television series *Lost in Space*: "Danger, Will Robinson. Danger!"

Makeup is one of those touchy areas that tends to be a big-win or big-lose situation. Apart from bad acting, few things are worse than bad makeup. Doubtless you've seen it for yourself . . . the young high school kid who looks every bit his age: hair made "gray" with baby powder and hair spray; dark, furrowed brow lines on his forehead and jowl lines on his lower cheek courtesy of someone's Magic Marker; and a dusting of powder to give that elderly "ashen" look.

What do you have? A cross between *Dawn of the Dead* and *Creature From the Black Lagoon* (sans facial hair).

Whatever the character is, he isn't old and all you notice throughout the entire performance are those silly black lines on his face.

Betcha he has to use a cane, too.

A rare scenario? Nah. It happens all the time.

A few simple rules of makeup could change everything . . .

1. The KISS principle applies here, as well. Start by learning to use a simple base makeup. Any good cosmetologist can help you with this. Or ask people in your church who do well with their own makeup (we hope that means some of the women).

The makeup most characters will need is simple: foundation on the skin, eyeliner on the eyes, blush on the cheeks, a touch of color on the lips, and light powder to ward off shine. This makeup adds color to your actors' faces and washes out those unsightly blemishes that appear on faces of teenage Hamlets and Ophelias who perform on a well-lighted stage. And don't let the guys try to get out of it; they need makeup on stage as well.

2. Use the necessary highlighting sparingly and tastefully. When you highlight actors' features to transform their appearance or age, use your common sense. Is the character ill? old? of a different nationality? Look at photos or people you know who are similar to the character. Note how shadows fall on their eyes, cheekbones and foreheads. Also note their neck and hands. (When applying makeup don't forget to cover all of the skin that is visible on stage. Don't simply apply makeup to the face and stop at the chin.) Try to recreate the effect you want with your base makeup.

Practice and experiment with makeup as much as time allows. Always strive for believable makeup so it adds to the character and enhances the play—not pulls everyone's attention away because they're trying to figure out how you'll ever manage to scrape off all that stuff.

There are many good books available on the use of makeup, many books we've listed in—yeah, you guessed it—the resource section. We've also listed a few wholesale makeup outlets that supply every imaginable type of theatrical makeup from eyebrow pencils to latex noses.

3. Always check the makeup under the lights you'll use for the performance. Often the look you'll get in the church restroom or back stage area isn't what you'll see on stage. When the actors think they've perfected their makeup, ask them, one at a time, to stand on stage under the lights you'll use for the performance. Have the others sit in the audience and critique the makeup. Is it realistic? Does the face contain the appropriate amount of color? Are the eyes well-defined? Are the neck and hands covered as well? What needs to be changed?

Make any necessary changes in makeup so the characters are as believable as possible.

Sorry, What Was That Again?

A wise old saying that we just made up is, "You can look great, act great, even sing great, but if the folks can't hear ya, put the cows in the barn, Martha, and head for home!"

We've already talked about the director's and actors' role in being heard by the audience but there's more to sound than that. As remarkable as the human ear is, many church buildings and auditoriums weren't built with it in mind (no pun intended). Sound is an area that is often the least obvious, yet the most important to quality productions. Good, audible voice amplification is critical to all productions no matter how simple or complex.

Very few buildings have natural acoustics good enough to perform without amplification. If people tell you their building has perfectly natural acoustics, they probably mean that a shouting preacher or a 200-year-old pipe organ can hold its own in the room. This sort of natural acoustics won't make it for most productions. A good sound system is an absolute for any crowd over 100 people and is highly recommended for smaller crowds.

If you don't already have a quality sound system, check with a professional for your specific circumstance. He or she can tell you what equipment you'll need for your production. If your production is worth doing, it's also worth hearing. Check your area phone book or the resource section for companies to contact for all your sound needs (speakers, amplifiers, mixing boards, etc.). Sometimes companies will lend sound equipment to non-profit productions in exchange for an advertisement in the program. It's worth a try. You also can call other churches or businesses in your area. They may have a quality sound system you can borrow. Always include an acknowledgment in your program for any assistance from others.

Recruit a volunteer to be in charge of sound for your rehearsals and production. It's best if this person has experience with sound. Ask people in your church, or recruit a person from the local high school theatre department.

Here are a few things you should know about microphones . . .

1. If at all financially possible, the best type of microphone for stage is a wireless lavalier system. These remote systems require no microphone cable and give the actor complete freedom of movement on stage. In addition, a quality lapel (lavalier) microphone is small and can be hidden fairly easily on a belt or under the actor's clothing without impeding the sound quality or amplification.

One major drawback to the use of a remote sound system is cost. If ever there was a product that holds true to the adage "you get what you pay for," it's a remote system. Some systems are reasonably priced, but our experience has shown that the less expensive systems don't hold up as well, particularly if you want to take your group on the road. These systems often don't possess things like channel diversity, which prevents your system from acting like an FM receiver for local radio stations. Cost for batteries can also become a major expenditure. The average alkaline battery life on a normal system is a maximum of four hours. If you have a number of microphones and do numerous performances, the cost of batteries will add up.

A minor drawback to remote systems is vocal reproduction quality during singing. The small remote microphones do phenomenally well on spoken parts but lack significant dynamic range when used in singing. We said this is a minor drawback because, first of all, major strides are being made by the manufacturers of these systems to improve this area. Secondly, the majority of your audience won't notice the difference between quality of speaking amplification and quality of singing amplification.

If you use a remote system for a production, prior to the show have someone check that all microphones have fresh batteries, that all receivers are plugged in, and that everything tests. (Sound check!)

When actors go off the stage, ask them to turn off their microphones; then the audience won't hear backstage whispering. Be sure to coach your actors to turn on their microphones when they go back on the stage, or for any offstage speaking parts.

2. An alternative to remote systems is to use regular microphones on stands. Here are a few general tips to keep in mind if you use them:

● Always make certain that the microphones are placed slightly below the mouth at an approximate 45-degree angle. This will allow for maximum sound. Set the height of the stand so that the actor can take a comfortable stance—not unnaturally erect or slouched.

● When positioning a microphone, depending on where the dialogue takes place, place it in favor of your performer's right or left. For example, if the actor is seated or standing and talking to someone on his or her right, have the actor stand slightly to the left of the microphone. Proper positions will determine how well the actors are heard. Obviously, if a monologue is delivered to the audience, the microphone should be centered with the mouth.

3. Never draw attention to the microphones. Always set up your microphones before the program starts, and only move them during a blackout. Don't let your performers fiddle with them, lean on them, or even look at them. If you give the visual idea that the microphones don't exist, the audience won't notice them as much. If for some reason a microphone must be moved or adjusted, do so without looking at it; reposition it quickly and fluidly. Only do this when you are already moving on stage and during someone else's lines. Coordinate such movement with your sound person so he or she will know to turn that particular microphone off before it is moved. We are all aware of the annoying crash, bang and boom that accompany moving a microphone.

4. Be careful of microphone cords. Be aware of the position of cords so as not to trip over them. After a microphone is in position, always shake any tangles out of the cord then pull it to the microphone stand so that the cord doesn't drape out away from the stand. (Moving the cords should be done during a blackout or as inconspicuously as possible.)

Let There Be Lights

Just as sound allows the actors to be heard, light allows them to be seen. Lighting can do more than that if you have the talent and facilities. Even a simple, well-constructed lighting system can turn an average presentation into a more effective performance.

Why?

Because . . .

1. Lighting establishes moods. Through very simple colors or combinations of colors (blue = cool, red = warm, etc.) you can immediately draw the audience into the right frame of mind for a scene. You can also convey tons of information to the audience about the setting: the time of day, the character or part of the stage on which the audience should focus, etc.

2. Lighting acts as a punctuation mark. When a sketch ends on a comic punch line, an immediate blackout serves as an "exclamation point" for the humor. It accentuates the suddenness of the punch line and clarifies that the sketch is over and it's time to laugh uproariously. Audiences are conditioned for this response. When the lights go out, the sketch or scene is over (whether it's supposed to be or not).

For more reflective or pensive endings, fade out the lights. This allows for the emotion to carry on for a thoughtful moment or two before moving on to the next sketch or act.

A Hint for Your Actors

When using a lighting system, never move on a blackout or fade until the lights are completely down and the actors have counted to three. The reason is simple: for the sake of production pacing. Many times we have an overwhelming desire to get off the stage, so we move before the lights are off. The audience sees us break character by moving in a way that has nothing to do with the play. The illusion is broken. It's no longer a character moving purposefully across the stage, but an actor scrambling to get to his or her next position. It reminds the audience that they're not really where we want them to believe they are; they're in an auditorium watching a bunch of actors. A count of three after the lights have gone down will help safeguard against this.

The Equipment

Check the references in the resource section for companies and equipment that'll get you what lighting equipment you'll need. (We thought we'd say it right at the top.)

But what equipment do you need?

Here's a quick overview of a few of the more widely used lights, and then you can decide:

● **The Fresnel light.** This light is useful because it can be adjusted to cover larger or smaller portions of your stage. It is especially good for downstage areas if you're hanging the lights from ceiling beams or scaffolding. The distance for this particular light is most effective at 25 or 30 feet.

● **The ellipsoidal light.** Commonly called a "Leko," this light is good for distances over 30 feet and has a flexible beam (because of how the light is constructed) with an intensity that matches spotlights of higher wattage. It is good for beams or upstage lighting. It can also be fitted with an iris to allow for varying sizes—sharp, round or whatever.

● **The follow spotlight.** This is what most of we non-technical illiterates generically call a "spotlight" or "follow spot." It handles distances from 75 to 125 feet or more and is constructed to cover large portions of the stage or zero in on a single moving performer. It can be helpful in dramatic productions but is more commonly used in comedy and musicals. (Because of their nature, comedies and musicals lend themselves to the more overt theatrics a follow spot can create.)

Thinking of Making Your Own Lights?

This can be a great money-saver if you have the people who know how to do it. But be sure to answer three obvious questions:

1. Is it electrically safe? If not . . . your audience might enjoy the special effects, but your church leadership will likely frown upon the church burning down.

2. Does it look good? Four flood lights painted blue and strapped to a board aren't "aesthetically appealing." Not only that—they will get more attention than your performers. If you're going to make your lights, do it right. Check the resource section for books on lighting, or contact an electrician from your church and enlist his or her help.

3. Are you using quality materials? Not only do four flood lights strapped to a board look bad, they do a lousy job. Lights should be constructed to contain the light they're emitting—not let it bleed throughout the room.

Set Construction

All sorts of factors affect set construction: how simple or elaborate your production is; whether you're performing on a stage where you can pound a few nails into the floor; whether you're in a church sanctuary where you can't touch a thing; or if you have the knowledge of carpentry and painting to make a set look good.

Some of the things we've already discussed in making lights apply here. If the sets you build are not going to look good, don't do it. If the sets will distract from the theme of the production, don't do it. If you think the sets are going to make up for deficiencies in acting, don't do it.

Because we're a couple of simple-minded guys, we prefer simple sets. Number one: They're easy. Simple sets let you focus on more important elements of the production. Number two: The majority of churches don't have the time, talent or facilities to make elaborate sets of good quality. Most attempts wind up looking horrible. Number three: Are the sets really that important to the success of your production?

If you're determined to give it the old college try, pick up the tools, lumber, canvas, and paint and delve into such terms as flats, toggle bars, keystones and crosspieces. Then turn the pages with us to that beloved land of invaluable references—yes, the resource section—and we'll get you help.

Promoting the Production

Okay, enough with the technical jargon for now. Let's turn our attention to another non-acting yet very vital area: publicity—getting the word out.

Depending on what kind of production you're presenting and who you want to reach, there are a number of good places to publicize. But first make certain that your outgoing information contains all of the following: Who is doing the production, what play or sketch they're performing, when they'll perform it, where they'll perform it, and how to get in to see it (through tickets, free admission, offering, etc.).

● **In the church.** As we've already mentioned, the first several outlets for publicity are easy for you to use: word of mouth, announcements in your church newsletter or bulletin, announcements from the pulpit and in various classes and youth group activities, and through other church mailings.

To separate your play or sketch from other events, make sure the advertisement stands out by looking stylish and appropriate to your production. You can publicize the production by performing a small part of it for a worship service or other church activity—just to give everyone a taste of what's coming. Also, ask your pastor to give an announcement about your production. A verbal announcement from your pastor with his or her personal endorsement will ensure an increased attendance.

● **Posters and fliers.** Create some nice, appropriate artwork, or take photos of the cast and put together a variety of posters and fliers—next to word of mouth, these are the oldest forms of publicity. Illustration 5 is a sample that can be used as a poster or flier.

Hang poster and fliers wherever the law allows: in shop windows or malls, on telephone poles or community bulletin boards, etc. Hand out fliers in the usual places where people gather. They are an effective means for reaching people outside your normal circles.

One note: Don't let your posters or fliers become part of the litter problem. After your production has ended, go back, take them down and clean them up. Otherwise, it's a pretty poor testimony of your church or group.

● **Press releases and articles.** Most large metropolitan, community, or town newspapers will accept press releases and articles about your production. They might not use them, but they'll accept them. Sometimes they'll take them "as is." What have you got to lose? Send an article about your production to the city editor. He or she may want to interview you further for a longer article.

Whenever possible, include a close-up photo of an interesting portion of your show. This will "class up" your press release and increase the chances of the article being printed.

Illustration 5
Poster or Flier

HOME AGAIN

A heartwarming play about the love of a family.

Sunday
November
15
7-9 p.m.

Performed
by King of
Glory Youth

Freewill
offering will be
collected

Nursery
provided

Besides that, most newspapers dedicate sections to free publicity for local events. Call your local newspaper for information about format and send it in! Many communities also have "shopper's guides" with free publicity for non-profit organizations. Ask around, maybe they can help you. If you have the money, you can always buy advertising space (often at a discount if you're non-profit).

For a better idea of a press release, take a look at Illustration 6.

Illustration 6
Press Release

● For immediate release

● Contact: _____
(name of person in charge of promotion, and phone number)

● "Local church youth group to present family program."

_____ youth group will present a
(name of church)

series of dramatic and humorous short sketches showing common

family struggles and tensions on _____, _____ at _____.
(day)   (date)   (time)

The sketches address the needs of teenagers and parents from a

Christian viewpoint. The program will be held at _____,
(place)

_____, _____
(address)   (city)

Senior high teenagers, their parents and youth leaders are encouraged
to attend. A nursery will be provided; admission is free.

● **Television and radio spots.** Though the Federal Communications Commission doesn't push public service announcements as much as it used to, most television and radio stations allow time for public service announcements for civic and religious groups. You can use Illustration 6 as a guide to write your own radio announcements. Stations will often produce them with background music or "live" through the disc jockey.

● **Other churches.** Don't forget to send a personal letter describing your program (along with posters and fliers) to other area churches and organizations. They're often the ones most interested in what you're doing and often the ones we forget to contact. Call the pastor or youth minister, if you can. Who knows? You might create some much-needed unity between your church and others.

● **Your program.** The idea behind printing a program for your performance is to let your audience in on what they're about to see and clarify any advance information they'll need to follow your production: time, setting, chronology of scenes, etc.

A program also is an opportunity to give credit where credit is due. List the name of the play; author; players; director; music director; and people in charge of lights, sound, makeup, costumes—anyone and everyone who contributed to the production. (Don't forget the individuals who provided refreshments or took care of the nursery for you. Or the people or businesses who provided you with props, set pieces, or anything that helped with the production.)

Never assume you know how to spell someone's name. Check all name spellings several times before and after the program has been typed. You wouldn't want to hurt or offend anyone who has contributed to the evening. Illustration 7 is a sample program. Use it as a guide when you prepare a program for your production.

A Publicity Checklist

To map out your time more effectively, here's a suggested publicity checklist for you to follow:

Six to Eight Weeks Prior to Your Production:

_____ Notify any monthly periodicals (local publications, school newspapers, magazines, etc.).

_____ Print posters and fliers.

Two to Three Weeks Prior to Your Production:

_____ Send posters and fliers with cover letters to other area pastors and youth leaders.

_____ Send press releases to local newspapers and shopper's guides.

_____ Include fliers in church bulletins for two or three consecutive Sundays.

_____ Send public service announcements to local radio and television stations.

_____ Place posters and fliers on community bulletin boards in banks, libraries, shopping centers, schools, etc.

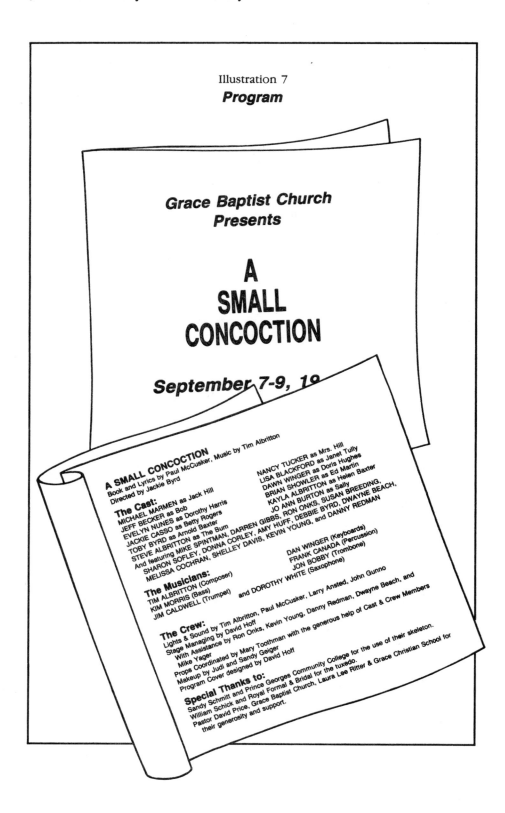

Illustration 7
Program

_____ Contact local Christian bookstores for placement of posters. Ask them to consider using your fliers as "shopping bag stuffers."

_____ Make a "VIP" invitation list. Send special invitations to church and community leaders who may not otherwise attend.

_____ Send posters to local colleges and high schools with music and theatre departments.

_____ Assemble and print your program.

Ten to 14 Days Prior to Your Production:

_____ Begin concentrated poster distribution and display to wherever you can put them.

_____ Have your group personally distribute fliers around the city at malls, shopping centers, schools, etc.

_____ Consider placing a banner or lighted sign in front of your church (or place of performance) announcing the production.

_____ Begin concentrated effort of prayer throughout your group and church, that your production will minister inside your church and work as a strong outreach to the community.

8
Rehearsals

(Getting to the Stage With Minimal Scars)

We can talk about directing and acting until the proverbial cows come home (an expression that has always made us wonder where the cows have been and why it's taken them so long to get back), but rehearsals need to be discussed before we go any farther in this book.

Be Prepared

Get your act together before you get the "acts" together (that's a show-biz phrase we just made up). Before you rehearse, here are some things you must do:

1. Reaffirm your goals and plans, and know how you want to carry them out.

2. Know exactly what you're going to do—who will be involved in what acts, scenes or sketches—so you'll use time efficiently. Never go into a rehearsal unprepared. If you do, it'll be a waste of time. Your cast will know it and you'll know it. Hand out an entire schedule for rehearsals—dates, times and places. Indicate which characters you'll be rehearsing with and at what times.

3. Know the material thoroughly. If you don't, the pressure of rehearsal (time, decision-making, input from the cast) will master you rather than the other way around.

4. Make sure you have all the material you need—scripts, schedules, etc.

5. Maintain a balanced frame of mind, one that will push to get things accomplished but also leave room for creative expression and input from your cast. The director must direct, but he or she can do so without being a tyrant.

6. Be realistic in your expectations, and articulate deadlines to the cast (for example, when lines should be memorized, etc.).

7. Prepare alternative plans for absenteeism and conflicting schedules.

8. Be prompt for all rehearsals. Arrive early enough to set everything up so you can begin when your cast arrives.

9. Don't assume anyone knows anything. Tell all cast and crew every possible detail.

10. Have some fun. Okay?

We've Only Just Begun . . . but When and How?

Figuring out when and how to schedule rehearsals will depend on the difficulty of the material; the experience of your cast; the availability of rehearsal space; competing church, school and youth group activities; and how often the members of your cast can rehearse.

When scheduling rehearsals the first thing to do is to determine the date of your opening night, and work backward from there. Once you determine the date of the opening performance, stick to it.

Remember: This ain't Broadway. Six weeks with five rehearsals each week might appear to be a good plan for you, but it may not be practical for your group. Face it, that's a lot of commitment for a group of unpaid amateurs. (But if they *want* to rehearse that much, then go ahead!)

However, you *will* need to have a good number of rehearsals to compensate for the lack of experience. Schedule the rehearsals close enough to avoid the ongoing problem of forgetting directions and lines from rehearsal to rehearsal. Also, run each rehearsal for at least two hours, and schedule it 15 minutes before you really plan to start—that's the magic amount of time for tardiness in classes, meetings, church services and other activities.

Here are general ideas for determining how much time you'll need between your first rehearsal and the opening performance:

1. The first few rehearsals should include reviewing general goals and plans for production; reading, discussing, analyzing and interpreting the material's content and characters; listening to the director's overall views and intentions; showing set designs, costume ideas, and sound and lighting plans. But, please be careful. Don't overwhelm your cast with too much in the first rehearsal. Many directors have the tendency, in genuine enthusiasm, to unload everything they want to do in the first five minutes of the first rehearsal. That wouldn't be so bad if the cast felt the same enthusiasm. Unfortunately, when this happens the cast usually feels overwhelmed. Don't make your goals bigger than they really are. Remember to go slowly—for the cast's sake and yours.

2. During the next few rehearsals cover blocking of the material, divided as needed by acts, scenes or individual sketches (depending on your production). Your actors should write notes of stage movements, character specifics, line delivery and other acting considerations about the material. This is the development process for what will ultimately become the program seen by your audience. Don't expect too much from your actors since they'll be concentrating on getting the basics down before they can polish their work. On larger productions, don't expect your cast to memorize any lines until you've finished blocking and clarified basic delivery.

3. In the next few rehearsals continue work on blocking with development and polish of characterization, line delivery and general movement—going over this at least twice each rehearsal. Bring the acts, scenes or sketches closer to the perfection needed for the opening night performance.

4. The next "section" of rehearsals involves running through the cumulative material—acts, scenes or sketches—incorporating everything you've done up to this point without scripts and with as few interruptions as possible.

5. Another section of rehearsals should incorporate a run-through of all the material including costumes, technical elements and anything else beyond previous rehearsals. Again, this should be done without scripts and with as few interruptions as possible.

Also in this section, include individual rehearsals for those parts of the production that need more attention: Coach individual actors, run through the program with the technical crew (without the actors) to ensure smooth-running dress rehearsals.

Inherent in any production is meeting with those in charge of costumes, makeup, technical aspects and publicity, to make sure everything is coming together as it should and to ward off potential problems. Plan for this at least once every other week (or more, if necessary). If you're the person in charge of all these things, then talk to yourself as much as you need to! And then you're ready for . . .

6. The first dress rehearsal. Have the actors run through the entire program as if they were performing for an audience. Make sure everything is as it should be. Do not forget to practice curtain calls! Interruptions should occur only if absolutely necessary. Make notes of problems, but wait until the end of the run-through before you mention the problems and get them corrected.

7. The second dress rehearsal. Again, the program should be run as if the actors were performing for an audience (and it's not a bad idea to have people in attendance). Continue working out any bugs in the production, questions and greater details.

8. The third dress rehearsal. Yeah, it might seem a bit excessive but you'll be glad you did. This should be it—everything exactly as it should be for opening night.

Rehearsals can evolve over a four- to 12-week period depending on you, your people and the amount of time you can put into the production. Here is a sample 10-week rehearsal schedule—one rehearsal a week. Use it as a guideline when you plan a rehearsal schedule to fit your own needs and time frame.

Rehearsal Schedule

Week One:
- Review rehearsal schedule and general production goals.
- Read through material as a group. Discuss, analyze and interpret content and characters.
- Ask actors to read the script more thoroughly on their own.

Week Two:
- Discuss basic needs for sets, costumes and props.
- Begin work on characterization and line delivery.

Week Three:
- Begin basic blocking. Have actors take notes on specific movement for their character.
- Continue work on characterization and line delivery. Stress the need of memorizing lines.

Week Four:
- Continue polishing blocking, characterization and line delivery.
- Have actors begin experimenting with makeup.
- Incorporate props as you acquire them.
- Work on making or borrowing sets and costumes.

Week Five:
- Include technical crew in rehearsal. Work on lights and sound.
- Continue developing and polishing blocking, line delivery, interaction with and reaction to other characters.
- Most lines should be memorized.

Week Six:
- Individual rehearsals for those parts of the production that need more attention: individual actors, technical, etc.
- Continue polishing all material.

Week Seven:
- Rough run-through of entire material incorporating everything you've done. Limit the interruptions.
- Keep experimenting with makeup. See what it looks like under the stage lights.
- All lines should be memorized.

Week Eight:
- First dress rehearsal. Run through entire program. Complete with makeup, costumes, props, sets, lighting and sound.
- Practice scene changes and movement of microphones (if necessary). Remember to make the changes smoothly and quietly. Keep the stage area clean.
- Practice covering for each others' mistakes.

Week Nine:
- Second dress rehearsal. Run through program; continue to

work out any problems.

Week 10:
● Third dress rehearsal. Final chance for polishing all aspects of the performance. Everything should run smoothly—set changes, costume changes, etc. Don't forget to practice the final curtain call.

A Specific Rehearsal Plan

Here's a suggested time schedule within each rehearsal:
● Start with prayer and then spend the first part of the rehearsal making announcements, handling business, and getting everyone warmed up. Do this through the exercises we've described in Chapter 5. Go over lines and review what's been done in previous rehearsals.
● During the next part of the rehearsal concentrate on new material to be learned. Take a quick break, if necessary.
● After the break, review what you've just done and then move into more detailed areas of practice; for example, with individual actors or scenes that might need intricate work.

For those actors not working with you on a scene or waiting for their time to come up, encourage them to spend the time learning lines; working on characterization; or helping with sets, costumes, makeup, etc.

Dealing With Your Actors

Even after you've done everything you can to select the right people with the right chemistry, you're still going to have some problems. Here are some typical examples of people you may have trouble with:

1. The power strugglers. Almost every cast will have one or two members who will try to take over in some subtle (and sometimes not-so-subtle) ways. They will automatically tell the other actors where to pick up their lines or tell them what to do. Sometimes they'll tell *you* what to do. If you see this happening, stop it at the beginning by privately explaining to them that you appreciate their help but would like them to relax a little. You are supposed to be in charge, after all.

2. The "I can't do it" people. These people believe they can't act because of shyness, self-consciousness, overall inhibitions or even moral reasons. Be patient and assuring with such people in public and then, if you have to, discuss it more thoroughly in private. Work toward a reasonable solution. If the attitude continues, gently warn them that you might have to get someone else to do the part.

3. The "I need to try it this way" people. Sometimes—just sometimes—you'll have actors who'll want to spend hours trying and retrying different things. Given half the chance, they'll monopolize entire rehearsals while searching for the perfect way to say a line or explore character. Keep a tight rein on this problem. Nothing is more boring or disruptive for the rest of the cast than to watch the director and an actor beat a rehearsal to death with a pretentious stick.

4. The "shy"sters. These are the people who are painfully shy, but for one reason or another try out for your production. Know in advance that they'll need a lot of encouragement and a lot of your time to warm up to the idea of going on stage. You can help extremely shy kids best by working with them one-on-one. Ask them to come 20 minutes early to each rehearsal for extra coaching. You also can work with them within the group doing the improvisations and exercises mentioned in Chapter 5. As the shy kids get used to working in front of the group it'll be less difficult for them to get in front of the audience. One warning: Your time and energy might not pay off. It is possible that you'll get to the opening performance and they'll "freeze up"—either before or after they're on stage.

5. The "hams." Most youth groups or churches have people who love to be in the spotlight on stage. They show no fear or inhibition. To a certain extent, these people are fun to work with. However, guard against focusing too much attention on the "hams" and too little attention on the ones who are more quiet and shy. The quiet ones will need coaching to overcome their inhibitions; the "hams" may need coaching to share the limelight.

Here are more things to consider when dealing with your cast:

● **Remain sensitive to your actors' egos and personalities.** Few activities make an individual feel more insecure or vulnerable than standing in front of a bunch of people and acting—unless the individual is a "ham" by nature. All problems or confrontations should be handled sensitively and privately.

● **Encourage individual actors.** Never assume people know they're doing a good job. Keep telling them. This doesn't mean to flatter indiscriminately or lie just to make someone feel good. Your comments must be constructive without being condescending.

● **Encourage the group as a whole.** Work toward a family unity so the actors feel like they're playing an important role no matter how small their part may be. Help them develop relationships with each other through social activities beyond rehearsals. (Be careful with male/female relationships. Nothing could be more damaging than to have a couple fall in love at the beginning of a production only to have them break up right before opening night—and then refuse to perform with each other.)

● **Always communicate in terms the cast will understand.** Work with them to ensure they're hearing correctly what you're saying. You'll be surprised at how semantics vary even in the same church.

● **Limit interruptions.** Help your actors maintain their character and sense of emotion by limiting distractions and keeping unnecessary people out of rehearsals (friends, family, etc.).

● **Be positive.** Never reveal your doubts and fears about the success of the production or the abilities of anyone involved. You can do incredible damage by voicing a doubt or negative feeling to the wrong person.

● **Videotape a couple of rehearsals.** Videotape trouble spots and then let the cast see themselves in action. It is extremely enlightening. Suddenly all the things you've been telling them will make sense because they're seeing themselves do it. Don't rely on videotape too much, though. It could actually damage performances and diminish the intuitive role of the director. (The director is the audience's eyes as well as their hearts. Producing a play requires intuition—an ability to *sense* what the audience will think, see and feel.)

● **Catch and correct all mistakes.** Practice makes perfect . . . or imperfect. Whatever your cast practices in rehearsal will wind up on stage. If you let mistakes go by consistently, those same mistakes will haunt you when the actors perform. That's why you have to practice everything.

If you're working on a comedy, practice the pauses where you expect the laughs to occur. This rule is easy to forget since the funny lines seem to become less funny the more you rehearse them. Sometimes you forget that the lines are supposed to be funny at all. But your audience won't because they're hearing the lines for the first time. Have your actors hold for the laughs. Tell them, "Yes, it feels awkward to hold still or remain silent while the audience is rolling in the aisles, but for the audience time has stood still." Practice pauses.

● **Work toward a perfect performance but practice for reality.** Your actors must know what to do and how to respond if a line is forgotten or dropped—either by their mistake or someone else's. They must know how to stay in character and even ad-lib if necessary, to get the show back on track. The natural thing for most people is to panic, freeze up completely and exclaim something completely out of character like, "Whoops!" or "We forgot something" or "You missed a line." The goal to impress upon the actors is to keep the audience from realizing that something has gone wrong.

The goal can be practiced during dress rehearsals when the actors should be proceeding as if they're in front of an audience. If people make mistakes and don't cover well, tell them so. Ask them what they will do if it happens in the real performance. Guide them to some possible alternatives; for example, they can cover an actor's forgotten line by saying the next line with moderate adaptation. Practice covering for each other's mistakes.

Key Rules for Dress Rehearsals

Dress rehearsals should be scheduled as close to the opening performance as possible. This means that the director must maintain control in the midst of last-minute insanity. Try to keep an environment that shelters your actors from the noise and confusion of the task at hand. Keep all distractions to an absolute minimum and limit interruptions to only those things that bring the rehearsal to a halt (like the stage catching on fire, that sort of thing). During dress rehearsals every pore in your body will want to stop midstream and tell the actors their mistakes, but it's wiser to take extensive notes and go over the mistakes with the appropriate people later.

The dress rehearsals are also the best times to go over some basic rules of performance etiquette that, coincidentally, we're about to give you.

Basic Rules of Performance Etiquette (What a Coincidence)

1. "The show must go on"—an overused expression, yes, but still a true one. There are no valid excuses for missing a performance other than being trampled by marauding elephants or attacked by a crazed mongoose (even these are poor excuses).

2. Treat every performance as if it is the only one, and treat every audience as if they were the most important audience you'll ever have—no matter how small or large. If a problem arises, never break out of character or let the audience know there is a problem.

3. Be ready to go on stage at least one hour before the performance.

4. Never leave the hearing range of the stage during a performance unless you are not going on again for the rest of the night. (We had one girl slip off for a drink of water and miss her cue by a good minute.)

5. No peeking. It is very unprofessional to peek out front or through stage scenery to look at the audience. Also, keep any distracting backstage lights, noise or talking from the audience.

6. Don't ever wander through the audience with your makeup or costume on or any semblance of your character intact. It will destroy the illusion you're trying to create.

7. The cast must respect members of the technical crew and stay out of their way so they can do their job. The success of the performance depends on this.

8. The crew must respect the cast and not distract actors from maintaining their characters, concentrating or establishing emotions. The success of the performance depends on this.

9. Personal problems or squabbles have no place backstage or on stage. Take them somewhere else after the production is finished.

10. Make sure you have a clear understanding of your responsibilities the opening performance and for subsequent performances.

The Time for the Opening Performance Arrives

Already?

Okay, quick . . . go over the following mental checklist:

● The programs are printed, the ushers are in place, the nurseries are stocked with plenty of clean diapers, the tickets are sold or the offering plates are dusted off, refreshments are ready for intermission.

● The stage . . . what about the stage? The props are in place, lights are working (bulbs are changed with extras ready just in case), sound is checking out as it should. Though you might be tempted, stay away from any last-minute fiddling with the technical elements—it'll make your crew nervous and distracted.

● And the cast? They are ready to go on stage at least an hour before the program starts, and in place five minutes before it starts. Go backstage and pray with the cast. Remind them of a few last-minute things like projecting to the back of the audience and holding for laughs. Assure them of your confidence in their abilities. Never, ever let on that you're scared out of your wits. (For future performances, during this time you can remind the actors of your support, give them a pep talk to help keep the energy up, remind them about polish, and tie up the loose ends you saw in the previous show. Beware of carelessness and the playing around that usually follow after opening performances.)

● Everything is ready. Now, go somewhere—sit down or pace in the back—and pray. The success of the production is out of your hands.

2
Evaluation

*('Dem Ol'
Post-Production
Blues and How
Did You Do?)*

Apart from the sudden and obligatory emotional collapse
that often occurs after the final curtain has gone down,
there are some things you have yet to do.

First and foremost, tell the cast and crew what a good job you
think they did—verbally and, if you can, through handwritten
notes. Save any constructive criticism for another, more appropriate time.

Second, talk with the people who have helped organize the
production and with the church leadership. Ask them to help you
evaluate the effectiveness of your program. (Give yourself a few
days before you evaluate so you'll have time to become objective
and everyone else will have time to gauge the "days-after" reaction from the church.)

Complimenting the cast and crew is easy, evaluating the production requires answering some serious questions.

The Serious Questions

1. Did you achieve all of the goals you set for yourself? the cast? the crew? the material? If not, what goals weren't achieved? Why or why not?

2. What did you learn from this production that you can apply to future productions?

3. How did the audience respond during the performance? Did they laugh when they were supposed to? Were they moved emotionally? Were they bored? In what ways did the production succeed with the audience? In what ways did it seem to fail?

4. What kind of post-production comments have you received from those who attended the performance? Were the comments positive or negative? What kind of comments could be applied to future productions?

5. What kind of attendance did you have? What age group seemed most represented? Were the ticket sales or offering income any indication of pleasure or displeasure with the production? Explain.

6. If an invitation to attend a Bible study or an invitation for counseling was given at the end of the production, did anyone respond? How many? Do you believe it is an indication of the quality of performance or message? Why or why not?

7. Was the material you performed a wise choice? Why or why not? What would you change about what you selected for future productions? What would you look for in future choices?

8. How well did the actors perform? How would you assess the quality of their performance as a whole? as individuals? Now that the production is over, who would you use again? Why?

9. Were the technical people competent? If not, what could have been improved? Would you use the same people again? Why or why not? Apply these questions to all elements of the non-acting crew: lights, sound, costumes, publicity, makeup, etc.

10. How would you evaluate the directing? What elements in the program could be attributed positively to the director? negatively? How could the elements change for future productions? Did the director accurately capture the meaning of the material? Was there a good balance between message and medium? Were there any glaring directorial mistakes? What was done well that should be considered in the future?

11. If you had to do the whole production over again, what would you change? (Other than your deodorant.)

12. If you're developing an ongoing drama and comedy group, what have you learned and how will you proceed from here?

These questions and more will come to mind and should be sufficiently scrutinized before you undertake another production—providing your brain and emotions will allow you to even consider the possibility of another production. Ever. Aw, come on . . . you know it was worth the effort.

And That's It

It seems as though there should be a conclusive end to this book, but there isn't. This is a beginning. From here, you can use the sketches we've included, develop your own ideas, have your own experiences, and—who knows? Maybe you'll be writing a book like this in a couple of years. If you do, that'll be fine. We'll probably buy a copy (unless you want to dedicate it to us and send a couple for free).

Regardless, we continue to believe that drama and comedy, properly used, can be powerful tools to bring glory and honor to the church.

PART 2
DOING IT

(20 Sketches)

Welcome to the Sketches Portion of Our Show

We tried to cover a variety of topics and emotions in this collection of 20 sketches—remembering the balance we've discussed throughout this book. Each sketch is followed by several discussion questions designed to help stimulate conversation (even controversy) within your youth group or with your audience. Or you can use them to help your actors better understand their parts. Here are some suggestions for using the sketches.

● **Discussion starters.** Use them for virtually any sort of gathering. For example, if you are starting a Bible study for your youth group, have several people perform "The Bible Study" (see page 169). After the sketch, ask the kids the questions. Apply the questions to your Bible study and to the goals the kids hope to accomplish.

● **Teaching supplements.** Perform a sketch for worship, special services or classes. For example, if your church celebrates Reformation Sunday, during the sermon portion of the worship perform "Luther" (see page 185). You could print the questions in the bulletin for the people to answer on their own.

● **Outreach.** Use the sketches with puppets, street ministries, coffee houses or other forms of outreach. The sketches are easily adaptable and can be done with minimal props and costumes.

● **Just for fun.** When you're starting drama and comedy in your youth group or church, remember to start small; for example, perform one of the following sketches to highlight a retreat theme. Then gradually combine these sketches for a drama revue, dinner playhouse or talent show. If you want to perform a longer play, see our listings in the resource section. Use your imagination and feel free to adapt the sketches and questions to fit your special situation.

(Note to directors: Some of the sketches will have to updated as per latest fads, movies, songs, etc. Also, you will occasionally see the word "beat" in parentheses. Unlike a pause which is just a dramatic hesitation in the line, a "beat" means to alter the tone and/or rhythm of the line when it is spoken.) Have fun!

The Two Complainers

I n this sketch we hear a conversation between an optimist and a pessimist, and see the role change that eventually takes place between them. (Appropriate for Thanksgiving.)

Characters

NANCY—A pessimist who spends all her time complaining.
PAUL—Has a more optimistic outlook, until he talks to Nancy.

Setting

Could take place anywhere. A bench or couple of chairs.

Lights up on Nancy sitting alone with a long face and slumped posture—obviously depressed. Paul enters energetically and speaks with enthusiasm as he sits down next to Nancy.

PAUL   Hi, Nancy, how're you doing today? Great day, isn't it?

NANCY   (Shrugs) Eh. So-so, I guess.

PAUL   So-so? It's beautiful out here.

NANCY   If you say so.

PAUL   What's wrong with you? You're acting a little depressed.

NANCY   (Sighs) Am I?

PAUL   Yes, you are. What's bothering you?

NANCY   Nothing. Nothing at all.

PAUL   Are you sure? I mean, you sure look like something's bothering you.

NANCY   I can't help it. It's a look I inherited from my mother.

PAUL   I've seen your mother and she doesn't look like that. Come on, what's wrong?

NANCY   (Irritated) There's nothing wrong! Just because my parents wouldn't let me have the car last night and I couldn't go to the football game! Dad said the brakes are bad. I don't believe it.

PAUL   He probably didn't want you to get killed. The game wasn't very good anyway.

NANCY   See? Even you got to go. They made me stay home to study geometry for that test this morning.

PAUL   Boy, that was a tough test. I wish my parents made me stay home to study. You probably got an A because you got to prepare for it. It's a good thing your parents are—

NANCY   Parents can be so cruel. And you know what else? Since I didn't go to the game, Fred sat next to Ann instead of me. She's such a flirt and Fred's such a sucker, they're probably going steady today.

PAUL   Well, Fred doesn't have a real good reputation. You're probably better off with someone else. (Trying to be positive) You know, it looks to me like—

NANCY   Then my sister ripped a big hole in the dress I was going to wear to the banquet Friday night. She got on one end and the dog got on the other and between the two of them . . . (She gestures with hands and makes a ripping noise) I'd like to have both of them put to sleep.

PAUL   Yeah, I think I know what you mean.

NANCY   Then Diane has been talking about me behind my back again. She says I've been trying to steal Don away from her. Can you imagine me trying to steal Don? (Paul nods his head up and down until she looks in his direction, and then he shakes it from side to side) He's so ugly.

PAUL   He is—isn't he? He has that big nose. I used to like him about five minutes ago.

NANCY   And while I was walking to school, I got a run in my hose so I had to go all the way home and change again which made me late for my first class. The teacher got real rude about it, too.

PAUL   Teachers can be jerks about the smallest things.

NANCY   (Looks at him surprised) Do you really think so?

PAUL   Yeah. I was two days late on a paper once, and they knocked a whole grade off of it. They can be real insensitive.

NANCY   Insensitive. Yeah. Right.

PAUL   And this morning I had to put gas in my dad's car. Can you believe it? He didn't have the courtesy to fill it up for me.

NANCY   Well . . . yeah. That's pretty inconsiderate. Maybe he was busy.

PAUL   He could have made time. And my mom's been nagging me about mowing the lawn. Good grief, it's not like she doesn't have two arms and two legs.

NANCY   She works, doesn't she? She probably gets tired.

PAUL   Yeah, but do you know what else?

NANCY   Paul . . . Paul . . .

PAUL   What?

NANCY   Has anyone ever told you that you have an attitude problem? You should be more grateful for what you have. (She stands and exits indignantly as Paul deadpans a look of bewilderment to the audience)

BLACKOUT (Curtain)

Discussion Questions

1. Have you ever felt like either one of these characters? If so, which one? Are you a complainer? If so, how do you react to people who aren't? If not, how do you feel when you're around people who are?

2. The point of this sketch seems to be that bad attitudes are often contagious. Do you find that to be true? Explain. Have you ever been in a situation similar to this one? How did it turn out?

3. Find verses in scripture that address the topic of complaining and thankfulness. (Look through Proverbs and Psalms.) What conclusions can you come to from these verses? As Christians, what should our attitudes be about complaining?

4. How can you apply what you've learned to your attitudes about homework? youth group activities? duties at home? relationships with parents? relationships with brothers and sisters?

Sketch 2

A Question of Love

In this sketch we hear two different perspectives about a relationship that ended.

Characters

STACY—Girlfriend who just experienced a breakup.
KELLY—Stacy's concerned friend.
JEFF—Boyfriend who just experienced a breakup.
BOB—Jeff's concerned friend.

Setting

A table in a library stage left, and a table in a student lounge stage right. Full lights can be used or two spots to highlight each side as focus of attention falls there.

Lights up on Stacy and Kelly at the library table on left, and Jeff and Bob at student lounge table on right. It should be obvious that they are oblivious to each other—especially since they are in separate locations. Stacy and Kelly are studying; Jeff and Bob are talking.

KELLY (Looks at Stacy for a moment, then speaks) Are you all right, Stacy?

STACY (Looks up from book) Huh?

KELLY   There's something wrong. What's wrong?

STACY   There's nothing wrong.

KELLY   I know you, Stacy, and there's something bothering you.

STACY   I'm reading a book. How can you know something's wrong when I'm reading a book?

KELLY   Because you haven't turned the page in 10 minutes.

STACY   (Looks at book, surprised) Oh.

KELLY   Is everything all right with Jeff?

STACY   (Long pause) No.

(Switch to Jeff and Bob who are in the middle of their conversation)

BOB   Wait a minute, Jeff. You're telling me you don't want to see Stacy anymore? You broke up?

JEFF   Yes! Are you dense? I just said we did, didn't I?

BOB   I don't get it. I thought you guys were doing good. You're like *the* couple around here. What happened?

JEFF   I don't know. Something's changed. I . . . I don't feel the same.

BOB   What happened?

(Switch to Stacy and Kelly)

STACY   We went out last Friday night like we always do. It was a normal night. We got some pizza and went to play miniature golf and—

KELLY   That's a normal night? You broke up out of boredom then.

STACY   Don't make jokes, Kelly.

KELLY   Sorry.

STACY   Everything was fine until we started to go home. We went up to Lookout Point to . . . to . . .

KELLY   Play checkers.

STACY I thought we were going to talk.

KELLY Talk? At Lookout Point? The only talk that happens up there is body language.

STACY But it's always been different for me and Jeff. We'd really go up to talk. (Kelly looks at her with disbelief, Stacy catches on) Really. (Kelly continues to look at her skeptically) Well, we may have done a little kissing but he's never tried to . . . to . . . (She lapses into an embarrassed, brooding silence)

KELLY He tried.

STACY (Slow to acknowledge) Yes. He did.

(Switch to Jeff and Bob)

JEFF How long have we been dating? What—half a year? I told her I loved her and everything. I mean, if two people love each other then . . . There are ways to express love, right? I thought we were thinking the same thing . . . feeling the same way, you know? I mean, she said once that she liked how I kissed. So we were at Lookout Point and, well, I got a little carried away. It's natural. It's normal. I'm only human, right? And . . . well . . . (Pause)

BOB Well what?

JEFF She said no.

(Switch to Stacy and Kelly)

STACY I said I wouldn't do it unless we were married.

KELLY How did he react?

STACY (Pauses, shrugs) All right, I thought. He said he wasn't surprised. I think he was a little frustrated, but he said he understood. He even agreed that it was the right thing to wait. He said he appreciated my willpower.

KELLY And that's it? No "but I love you and want to share myself with you"? Or the now-classic "if you love me you'll let me"? None of those?

STACY No. He took me home. I thought everything was fine.

(Switch to Jeff and Bob)

JEFF   I respect her, Bob, I really do.

BOB   Yeah? Then why'd you break up with her?

JEFF   See, I got up Saturday morning and—well, I don't know. Somehow it felt different for me. We were supposed to go to the lake that afternoon and I just didn't feel like going. I went anyway. And that's when it happened.

(Switch to Stacy and Kelly)

STACY   He was completely different toward me. I could sense it. He didn't hold my hand or do all the little things I'm used to when we're together. So I asked him what was wrong. He hedged at first and then he . . . (Pauses, on the verge of getting upset, regains control) He told me he didn't think he loved me anymore. He said the feelings weren't there.

KELLY   What a jerk.

(Switch to Jeff and Bob)

JEFF   What a pain. She started crying and asking me all kinds of questions like "Why not?" and all that stuff, and I don't know any of those answers. It just went away. Who am I—Sigmund Freud? I don't know why it went away.

BOB   You don't?

JEFF   No.

BOB   Maybe it had something to do with what happened Friday night. Or what *didn't* happen.

JEFF   Oh, come on. It had nothing to do with that.

(Switch to Stacy and Kelly)

KELLY   It had everything to do with that! Stacy, open your eyes. He loved you up until Friday night and on Saturday it suddenly disappears? Excuse me, but I don't think love works that way. Not real love. "Jerk" is too nice a name. You're better off without him.

STACY   But . . . it hurts, Kelly.

KELLY It will for a while but then it goes away.

STACY I don't want to lose him. I . . .

KELLY Stacy . . .

STACY I've been thinking that maybe . . .

KELLY No. Don't say it.

STACY Maybe that's how to prove it. I should have done what he wanted. I love him, Kelly.

(Kelly stares at her, stunned)

(Switch to Jeff and Bob)

JEFF So, it's over. That's the way it happens sometimes. It'll be awkward for awhile but . . . we'll get over it. There are plenty of other fish in the aquarium. Maybe next time the love will last.

BOB Yeah . . . maybe next time.

BLACKOUT (Curtain)

Discussion Questions

1. What did you think of Stacy and Jeff's situation—both at Lookout Point and its result? Do you relate to their experience? How? Did Jeff do the right thing? Why or why not? Did Stacy do the right thing? Why or why not?

2. In your own words, define "love." Is love only a feeling? How can we demonstrate love to each other? to your family? friends? boyfriend or girlfriend?

3. What does the Bible say about love between a man and a woman? How is that love demonstrated? (For example, read 1 Corinthians 13.)

4. Is physical affection or sex necessary for showing love? What kinds of guidelines does the Bible give about physical affection? (In other words, how far should you go if you're not married?)

Sketch 3

Going Out

In this sketch a young couple leave for a date, but don't know where to go or what to do.

Characters

DAVID—The boyfriend.
JANE—The girlfriend.

Setting

Two chairs to represent David's car.

Lights up on the two chairs. David walks Jane to her side of the car and opens the door for her. She "gets in" as David walks around to his side and gets in.

DAVID   Okay, before I start the engine, let's decide where we're going. I don't want to waste a lot of gas driving around.

JANE   Okay. What do you want to do?

DAVID   I dunno . . . what do you want to do?

JANE   Whatever you want. It doesn't matter to me.

DAVID   I'd be happy to go wherever you want.

JANE   No, really, it's completely up to you.

DAVID   Why do I always have to decide? You decide for once.

JANE   I'm not going to decide. You're the man, you're supposed to decide. The Bible says so.

DAVID   Where does it say that?

JANE   Paul says it in Ephesians somewhere. So decide.

DAVID   That's only if you're married and we're not married. (Under his breath) Though it seems like it sometimes.

JANE   I heard that! You're not happy with our relationship?

DAVID   Yes! Yes! I am overjoyed with our relationship. Now will you tell me where you want to go?

JANE   (Pouting) You're not happy.

DAVID   I am. Honest I am. (Smiling at her toothily and points to his mouth as he tries to speak) See how happy I am? Now, where do you want to go?

JANE   I told you . . . you have to decide.

DAVID   (Moans) I thought these were the days of liberated women.

JANE   What's playing at the movies?

DAVID   Movies? We've seen everything worth seeing. Unless you want to go see the new Spielberg movie "E.T.'s Close Encounter With a Jaws That Was Colored Purple."

JANE   What about that new Disney film—the one about the dog from outer space?

DAVID   What's it called?

JANE   "The Dog From Outer Space."

DAVID   How original. Isn't there anything interesting to do?

JANE   Such as?

DAVID   What's going on at the church? Surely something fun is happening.

JANE   Well . . . the junior high group is going roller-skating.

DAVID   Nah. They'll kill us on the curves.

JANE   The senior high is going to a Christian rock concert.

DAVID   What's the name of the group?

JANE   The Bloody Martyrs.

DAVID   Forget it. They get their name from making ears bleed.

JANE   The college-and-career group is having a Christian aerobics class . . . The Sweaty Saints, I think they're calling it.

DAVID   Sounds like a great way to spend a Friday night. What else?

JANE   Well, the singles are mingling, and the marrieds are masquerading.

DAVID   Huh?

JANE   A costume party.

DAVID   This is ridiculous.

JANE   We could always do some serious lip-locking.

(David looks at her shocked)

JANE   Just kidding.

(David rolls his eyes)

JANE   Who says we always have to do something on a Friday night?

DAVID   Nobody. But . . . but that's what Friday nights are for— to do something. It's what I spend all week waiting for.

JANE   You spend all week waiting for this?

DAVID   Not this. I mean, this is the pits.

JANE   Aren't you happy just to be with me?

DAVID   Are you starting that happy business again? I'm happy, all right?

JANE   You don't have to get snippy.

DAVID   I'm sorry. It's just that this is absurd. We're tired of movies, television is mindless, the parks are all closed, the church is doing everything we don't want to do, and it's the same old thing everywhere else. What are we supposed to do?

JANE   We could always stay home.

DAVID   And do what?

JANE   I have a Bible study lesson I need to do for church on Sunday.

DAVID   You want to stay home on Friday night and study your Bible?

JANE   Think of it, David . . . we could study our Bibles together, maybe pray together, share some deep inner spiritual truths that we don't know about each other, and possibly grow and cultivate a whole new realm of spiritual existence for ourselves! What do you think? Huh?

DAVID   (Looking at first as if it sounds feasible, then . . .) Nah.

JANE   I didn't think so.

(Long pause)

DAVID   So what do you want to do tonight?

JANE   I dunno . . . what do you want to do?

(Lights fade to blackout)

Discussion Questions

1. Have you ever experienced a similar situation as this couple (not only as part of a couple but as friends going out)? If so, how did you resolve the problem? If not, what do you think this couple should do—what advice would you give them?

2. Come up with a creative list of activities you think this couple could have done.

3. What do you usually do on a Friday or Saturday night? Do we put a lot of pressure on ourselves to "always do something" on a Friday or Saturday night? Why or why not? How has the pressure harmed us, if at all? How does it help us?

Sketch 4

The Sit-In

I n this sketch a group of teenagers protest the church's "meaningless curriculum" by staging a sit-in on the church steps.

Characters

PASTOR LINDSEY—The long-suffering pastor.
DON—The leader of the "revolution."
ADELE—The assistant leader.

Setting

Pastor's office. Three chairs. Beyond that, a desk, books, office decorations, etc. could be used but not necessary.

Lights up on Pastor Lindsey's office. Don (wearing sunglasses) and Adele enter first, Pastor Lindsey follows.

PASTOR   (Gesturing to chairs) Sit down.

DON   Getting bossy won't help.

PASTOR   Sit down, *please.* (Don sits down) Where are your manners? You should let the young lady have a seat.

DON   That's no lady—it's just Adele.

(Pastor rolls his eyes and sits down—at his desk, if one is available)

ADELE   That's all right. I've been sitting for quite awhile.

PASTOR   All morning, as a matter of fact. On the front steps of the church, as a matter of fact. With 50 other kids. What do you think you're doing?

DON   (Taking off sunglasses) Protesting!

PASTOR   Protesting! You think this is the '60s?

DON   This form of protesting is just as valid now as it was then.

PASTOR   This is a church, not a college campus.

DON   You teach here, don't you?

PASTOR   Yes, but—

DON   This is a revolution. The youth group is revolting.

PASTOR   Some of the church leaders think so.

ADELE   We're staging this sit-in to protest the meaningless curriculum we're forced to endure every Sunday morning in Sunday school. And we're going to stay there until our demands are met.

PASTOR   Demands!

ADELE   Yeah. Lay it on him, Don.

DON   (Pulls crumpled paper from his back pocket) First thing we want is (Reads) a biology exam.

(Pastor and Adele look at him confused)

ADELE   Biology exam!

DON   (Embarrassed) Whoops. That's tonight's homework. (Pulls out another piece of paper—very large—that unfolds down to the floor. Pastor looks incredulously) Here it is.

ADELE   Hurry up. I don't want my seat on the steps to get cold.

DON   We want first a whole new curriculum for Sunday school—something that applies the Bible to our daily lives. We're tired of the ancient drivel we're being taught.

PASTOR	For example?
ADELE	Come on, Pastor, our lesson books are from the '50s. The needs of youth have changed since then. We can't relate to biblical perspectives on greased-back hair, the evils of Bill Haley and the Comets, or nylon jumps.
PASTOR	Nylon jumps?
DON	Sock hops.
PASTOR	What do you suggest?
DON	Updated training materials. It's a whole new generation you have here. (Reading again) We want classes on mind expansion through spiritual medication.
ADELE	Medi—tation, not medication. We're not into drugs.
DON	Sorry. It was a typo.
ADELE	Forget the list. We know what we want. We want classes on human dynamics and interpersonal communication.
DON	We want a class on the spiritual significance of Kafka.
PASTOR	Who?
ADELE	And that's just the beginning.
PASTOR	Somehow I suspected.
DON	We want encounter groups—with mandatory attendance by the church leaders.
PASTOR	Oh? Would you like a hot tub with that?
DON	Could you get one?
PASTOR	I'll see what I can do.
ADELE	Forget that. Just get us a Coke machine and pizza socials every Friday night.
PASTOR	Anything else?
DON	We want . . . (Trying to remember, looks to Adele, then remembers) Oh yeah, we want housing for the poor and food for the needy, too.

ADELE   And peace on earth.

DON   Yeah, peace on earth.

PASTOR   Obviously you've prioritized this list. Is that it?

(Don and Adele look at each other)

DON   Yeah.

ADELE   I think it'll do for now.

DON   Why? Can you think of something we missed?

PASTOR   No.

ADELE   So, what's your answer? Do we get what we want or do we sit on the steps until we rot?

PASTOR   Let's see . . . (Speaks slowly, striving to be diplomatic) Your complaints about the curriculum are justified. Even the Sunday school board feels that it is outdated and they have begun work on changes. I doubt, however, that they will go along with your suggested alternatives. I'm not so sure how *scriptural* mind expansion and encounter groups in a hot tub would be.

DON   (Standing) Back to the steps.

PASTOR   Hold on. I'm sure a compromise can be worked out.

ADELE   (To Don) I knew he'd say that. Didn't I tell you he'd say that? (To the pastor) What about the rest of the demands?

PASTOR   I'll . . . I'll have to speak with some other church leaders.

ADELE   You're giving us the runaround. Back to the steps! (She turns and marches off) You had your chance. (Exits)

DON   It's going to get nasty out there. (Puts on sunglasses with deliberate dramatic movement) We're talking about some serious sitting! (Turns, moves to exit)

PASTOR   Son . . . (Don turns to him) What should I tell your mom about dinner?

DON   Aw, Dad . . . this is a protest! I don't have time to eat.

PASTOR   You're right. Never mind.

DON   (Pause) What are we having?

PASTOR   Lasagna.

DON   Well . . . go ahead and set me a place. But I can't promise I'll be there. I'm not supposed to eat with the establishment.

PASTOR   Fine. We'll set a place for Adele, too.

DON   Okay. See ya. (Exits)

PASTOR   Bye, son. Have a good day. (Sighs, speaks to himself) It's tough being the father of a preacher's kid.

BLACKOUT (Curtain)

Discussion Questions

1. Though "sit-ins" and other similar forms of youth protest seem outdated now, how can you or your youth group get the attention of church leadership about things you believe should be changed? What constructive ways can change be suggested? What is your responsibility, according to scripture, if the leadership doesn't agree with the changes you propose?

2. What do you think of the list of demands presented in the sketch? If you were to approach your church leadership with a list of demands, what would it consist of?

Sketch 5

The Job Applicant

In this sketch a young lady puts in an application to become an adult.

Characters

GOWERS—The employment agency representative. Should be dressed very businesslike, no-nonsense attitude, yet friendly. (Can be male or female.)

BRENDA—A teenage applicant. Caught up in her youthful attitudes.

LOVELAND—An adult applicant. (Can be male or female.)

Setting

An office (two chairs) and a wastebasket.

Lights up on the office. Mr. Gowers is sitting in his chair taking notes on a clipboard. Brenda enters. He rises to greet her.

GOWERS   Come in . . . (Looks at clipboard for her name) Brenda. Please sit down.

BRENDA   Okay. (She sits down) It said in the paper that you could help me.

GOWERS   We'll try. Our motto here at the Acme Employment Agency is: "Whatever you can do, we'll find a spot

---

for you." Anything at all. It's guaranteed or your money back.

BRENDA You better. I'm getting pretty impatient. I've been at this for at least six years.

GOWERS What is it that you want to be? (During their conversation, he takes notes diligently)

BRENDA An adult.

GOWERS (Pause) Pardon me?

BRENDA An adult. You know: a grown-up.

GOWERS An adult? (Begins flipping through pages on clipboard) I don't know if I have a form for that.

BRENDA You said it was guaranteed.

GOWERS Yes! Yes! Of course it is. But . . . well, boy, that could be a toughie. Everyone wants to get into that these days. Let me get a few preliminary questions out of the way here and we'll see. How old are you?

BRENDA Sixteen.

GOWERS And what kind of qualifications do you have?

BRENDA Qualifications?

GOWERS Practical experience.

BRENDA Are you kidding? I survived puberty [or, junior high]!

GOWERS Yes. But how have you utilized your experience— your youth—to qualify as an adult? You need to give me some practical highlights.

BRENDA Well . . . I've learned how to look like an adult. When I was 15 I could get into bars and R-rated movies and places like that. Don't you think I look like an adult?

GOWERS You certainly do. But I've got 12-year-olds in here that can do that. All you kids look older these days. I need something more substantial. More . . . impressive. What have you done? What do you know?

BRENDA	Know? You're joking. I know plenty.
GOWERS	Like what?
BRENDA	I have a lot of knowledge in retail, economics and high finance.
GOWERS	(Impressed) You do!
BRENDA	Yep. I use my mom's credit card at the mall every weekend.
GOWERS	I see. High finance.
BRENDA	You better believe it. Oh—and I know about anatomy. I can tell you anything you need to know about pimples and unwanted body hair.
GOWERS	(Writing) Anatomy.
BRENDA	I can also tell you how many calories are in the candy bars and cookies I eat. And I dissected a frog once without getting sick.
GOWERS	(Scribbling on his paper) Okay, so you've picked up some practical knowledge in the math and sciences. How about literature and the arts?
BRENDA	I read all the latest fashion magazines and I know all the words to the most popular songs. The cool stuff—not the bubble-gum trash.
GOWERS	(Writing) Cool stuff. Any experience in psychology or sociology?
BRENDA	I know how to make my parents feel guilty when they punish me. I know how to get them to buy me makeup and dresses I don't need.
GOWERS	How are you at things like time management?
BRENDA	Time management? I know how to drive my brother to the baseball practice, meet my boyfriend at the mall, eat a hamburger, see a movie, and pick up my brother again and still have time to watch my favorite soap opera.
GOWERS	Organizational skills?

BRENDA   I've figured out how to fit everything under my bed so Mom thinks my room is clean. I'll bet you know a lot of adults who can't do that!

GOWERS   Most adults don't have to. That's what garages are for. Anything else?

BRENDA   I know how to skip my classes without my parents finding out. I know how to write essays so it sounds like I know what I'm talking about. And I know how to peek on final exams without the teacher seeing me.

GOWERS   I understand. Anything religious in your background?

BRENDA   I go to church.

GOWERS   Okay . . . what have you learned there?

BRENDA   I've learned how to pass notes to my friends without the pastor noticing. And I know how to give all the right answers when my Sunday school teacher asks me a question.

GOWERS   Oh?

BRENDA   Yeah, I just say "because the Bible says so" or "because Jesus died on the cross for my sins." That'll answer most of them.

GOWERS   Fine. So much for spiritual values. Do you have any technical skills?

BRENDA   We don't need them at church.

GOWERS   Not at church. In general.

BRENDA   I can work my radio, curling iron, television and telephone all at the same time. I can do my own makeup, too. (Points to her face) See?

GOWERS   (Looks) Great. Ringling Brothers might be interested. How are you at taking care of yourself? Are you self-sufficient?

BRENDA   I know how to stick a sock down my brother's throat when he needs it.

GOWERS   I mean financially.

BRENDA   I've got an allowance that I do pretty well with. I've got my parents convinced that they're failures as parents if they don't give me a lot of money.

GOWERS   I see. Do you have any references?

BRENDA   My best friend Barbara will talk to you—if we're still on speaking terms. She's mad at me because John Allison likes me instead of her.

GOWERS   Anybody else?

BRENDA   Bill—he's my boyfriend—he could tell you a lot.

GOWERS   That's what I'm afraid of. Anybody older?

BRENDA   Nobody older likes me.

GOWERS   Oh. (Writes a couple of final notes) Well, Brenda, I think that covers all the areas we need. You're looking to be an adult with a background of youth spent on nothing but self-centered pleasure seeking and blatant manipulation. Is that correct?

BRENDA   Sounds good to me.

GOWERS   No promises—but I'll see what I can do. With a little more experience, I'm sure you'll be an adult in no time. Okay?

BRENDA   Not too much longer, I hope. I want to hurry up and get out of the house. My parents are driving me nuts. (Beat) Is that it?

GOWERS   (Stands) I have all the information I need right here which will go in with the appropriate files. Thank you for coming by. (Extends hand to shake)

BRENDA   Nails haven't dried. (Stands)

GOWERS   Oh. Sorry.

BRENDA   No problem. See ya. (She exits)

GOWERS   Boy, these kids have gotten so job-specific these days. It'd be nice to hear from someone who just wants to be a fireman or a computer programmer or something easy.

(An adult applicant enters)

LOVELAND   Mr. Gowers?

GOWERS   Ah . . . (Checks name on clipboard) Chris Loveland. What can I do for you? Wait—don't tell me—you want to be president of a company.

LOVELAND   Actually, I want to recapture the lost innocence of my youth. You guys are guaranteed, right?

(Gowers looks to audience, deadpan expression on his face)

BLACKOUT (Curtain)

Discussion Questions

1. What do you think of Brenda? Is she qualified to become an adult? Do you think her attitudes and "experience" are typical of your friends and other young people you know? Do you share some of those same attitudes? If anything, what's wrong with her attitudes? What attitudes do you find most dangerous?

2. What qualifies a person to be an adult? Is it necessarily a matter of age or are other qualifications involved? If other qualifications are involved, what are they?

3. What qualities would you like to have as an adult? List them specifically. Do you see those qualities in most adults you know? If not, why do you think they lack them?

Sketch 6

A Father and Son

In this sketch a father gives his departing son some advice. (Appropriate for Father's Day.)

Characters

THE FATHER—The "imparter" of wisdom.
THE SON—The receiver of wisdom.

Setting

Their front porch. Bench or two chairs.

Lights up as the son enters with suitcase, sets it down and begins searching pockets for his car keys. Father enters.

FATHER	Is that the last of it?
SON	(Gestures to suitcase) That's it. Now all I have to do is remember what I did with my car keys.
FATHER	Son . . . before you go . . . I was wondering if we could have a little talk.
SON	If it's the birds and the bees talk, I already know.
FATHER	You do? Who told you?
SON	Mom.

FATHER   But you weren't supposed to know until you reached the age of 18. I told your mother that explicitly.

SON   Dad . . . I'm 20.

FATHER   Oh. (Beat) That's all right. It's not what I wanted to talk to you about anyway.

SON   Okay. I'm listening.

FATHER   You're moving out into the real world, Jimmy, and . . .

SON   Johnny.

FATHER   Huh?

SON   Johnny. Jimmy moved out last year.

FATHER   Oh. (Beat) I wonder if I had this talk with him, too?

SON   I doubt it. You were away on business when he moved out.

FATHER   That's right, I was. Well, son, you're moving out into the real world and you've got to be very careful. You're going to meet all kinds of people and get caught up in some very precarious situations.

SON   That already happened in high school.

FATHER   It did?

SON   Yes.

FATHER   Where was I?

SON   I think you were mowing the lawn.

FATHER   Somebody should have come and told me.

SON   We would have but you know how loud the lawn mower is.

FATHER   That's it—I'm buying one of those quiet electric types.

SON   Was there any other fatherly advice you wanted to give me, Dad?

FATHER   No, I don't suppose so.

SON   Well . . . thanks, Dad. I'll always remember what

you've told me here today. (Starts to pick up suitcase)

FATHER   Choices. I was going to say something about choices.

SON   I beg your pardon?

FATHER   When I was getting ready to move out of my house, your grandfather gave me some parting words about choices. He said, "Son, you're going to have to make choices. Lots of them."

SON   And what did you say?

FATHER   I said, "You're right, Pop." Disagreeing with him could be hazardous to your health.

SON   So you thought you'd carry on the tradition and tell me the same thing.

FATHER   Sort of. It has a certain poetic justice to it. See, you won't have your mother and me there to tell you the right way to choose. You'll be on your own. Your own man. A small, fragile child lost in a giant jungle. A tiny speck . . .

SON   What are you trying to say, Dad?

FATHER   What am I trying to say? (Beat, as if trying to remember) What am I trying to say? (Beat) What I'm trying to say is that one choice you must make daily is who you're going to serve.

SON   I work with computers, Dad. I'm not a waiter.

FATHER   I'm talking in the spiritual son, sense. (Corrects himself) The spiritual sense, son. You can serve yourself, money, Satan, God or just about anything.

SON   You're right.

FATHER   Even if you decide not to choose, you've made a choice. You're always going to serve someone. Remember that. I hope that your mother and I have instilled in you the desire to make the right choice.

SON   You have. Don't worry.

FATHER   I'm not worried. Your mother asked me to do this.

SON   She did? But she told me all this herself last week.

FATHER   Really? You're kidding. Why does she keep doing that?

SON   Thanks, Dad. It meant a lot more coming from you. I enjoy these father-and-son chats. We should do it more often.

FATHER   I would—if your mother would quit beating me to it.

SON   Well . . . I have to go. (Begins searching pockets) I can't imagine what I did with my—(Pulls out keys) keys.

FATHER   I'm going to miss you, son.

(There is a moment of silence)

SON   Do you think we should hug or something?

FATHER   It would make a nice Father's Day [Or going away] present, yes.

(They embrace)

SON   (Picks up suitcase, moves to exit) See you later, Dad. Thanks for the advice.

FATHER   Did I really give you any?

SON   Sure. And I'll be sure to pass it on to my son, too. See you in three days. (He moves to exit)

FATHER   See you later, Jimmy.

SON   Johnny.

FATHER   You, too. (Beat, realization) Three days? What do you mean "three days"?

SON   I'm just going for a weekend trip. (Exits) Bye.

FATHER   (Confused, speaks after he has gone) But I rented your room out!

BLACKOUT (Curtain)

Discussion Questions

1. How do you perceive the relationship between this father and son? Is it a good one? Why or why not? How could it be improved?

2. Describe your relationship with your parents. Is it a good one? Why or why not? How could it be improved?

3. Describe your relationship with your heavenly Father. Is it a good one? Why or why not? How could it be improved?

4. What do you think of the father's advice to his son? Is it sound advice? Do you believe that "you're always going to serve someone"? Is there scripture to support this advice? If so, what is it and what does it say?

5. Think of your own life. Whom do you serve? Is this a conscious choice you're making or does it just "seem to happen"? If it is a conscious choice, are you happy with it? Is it the right choice according to principles found in the Bible? If it just "seems to happen," how can you control it to become your own choice?

Sketch 7

A Phone Call From Elizabeth

I n this sketch the mother of John the Baptist decides to give him a call.

Characters

ELIZABETH—Should be played as a stereotypical Hebrew mother.

Setting

Elizabeth's living room with a phone. As simple or imaginative as you want to make it.

As lights come up, Elizabeth is moving to the phone, talking as if conversing with someone she's left offstage. As she talks, she picks up the phone and dials.

ELIZABETH　　It's getting out of hand, I tell you. Completely out of hand. He's your son, Zechariah, and what do you do? Are you listening to me, Zach? Answer me. (No answer) I didn't think so. I know you can talk to me—that old "can't talk because of God" excuse doesn't work with me. You got back your ability to speak a long time ago . . .

(Puts receiver to her ear) Hello, John? Son? Yes, it's your mother. Remember me? Elizabeth, the wife of your father. John, John—can we talk? John, it's your lifestyle. Now don't get me wrong, I'm only your mother, and I know you're pretty headstrong. But, John, I'm concerned about this business of living in the desert. Is that healthy? I've got a nice room right here for you and you're out with cactus and scorpions. I ask you. It must take all your money for suntan lotions and dust rags. I mean, John, really. What kind of life is that? It can't be very clean . . . (Pause) Oh. You spend a lot of time in the Jordan River. Great. You're trading dust for mud . . .

John, please, I hear people talk. A fashionable dresser you're not, I know. But . . . can we talk? Camel's hair and a leather belt, John. That's what they're saying . . . (Pause) Oh. It's true. Well, maybe it'll start a trend. Stranger things have happened . . .

I'm worried about you, John. I really am. The long hair. The beard. People get the wrong idea. Are you healthy? I mean, what are you eating these days? (Pause) Locusts. What is that—a nickname for some kind of Chinese food? (Pause) Oh. *Real* locusts. You're telling me you're eating bugs, John. I'm your mother, how can I be happy about that? Oh, you eat them with honey. Well, that makes me feel much better . . .

John, I have to tell you: I'm concerned about the comments you've been making . . . (Pauses) You know the ones—about the king and his wife? You're not being terribly diplomatic . . . (Pauses, holds phone away from ear for a second then holds it close again)

John . . . John . . . don't start that fire and brimstone stuff with me. I'm your mother. I changed your diapers before you covered them with camel hair. I'm not asking you to compromise your message. I'm just saying that there are more tactful ways of communicating. Phrases like "brood of vipers" just don't endear one to the populace, if you know what I'm saying. It's not the way to win friends and influence people . . .

John, are you listening to me? I'm worried. Forgive a mother for worrying about her only child. But I'm hearing things about the king and . . . well, he's not real happy with you. And I don't mean mildly annoyed either. Do you understand what I'm saying? . . .

(Pauses, tone changes, becomes softer) John, listen to me. When you were a child, I knew God had some special things in mind for you but . . . (Pause) John, I'm afraid. (Pause) I know about your mission, John. (Pause) I know you have to do what God commands. (Pause, getting upset) I know all about the sins of this generation, John, but I don't care about this generation. I care about you because you're my son. You're my miracle, John. (Long pause) Yes, son. (Pause) Yes. I won't keep you. (She slowly moves the receiver away from her face) I love you, John. (She slowly places it on the cradle and walks away. Exits)

BLACKOUT (Curtain)

Discussion Questions

1. As best as you can, outline what you know about the life of John the Baptist. What circumstances surrounded his birth? What seemed to be the purpose of his ministry? How did he die? (Check the Gospels, Bible concordances and dictionaries.)

2. What do you think about Elizabeth's feelings versus John's mission? Do you think Elizabeth's feelings could be reconciled with the purpose of John's mission? How?

3. John's mission had serious ramifications in the public eye and the king's thinking, as John's message was not always delivered with "diplomacy." Do you think John should have approached his "message delivery" differently? If so, how should he have changed? How do you think such a style of preaching would be accepted now? Explain.

4. How do John the Baptist's life and message affect your life at home? at school? at church?

Sketch 8

The Christmas Store

(With gratitude to David Hoff)

I n this sketch we visit a Christmas store that has little to do with the *Christ* in *Christ*mas.

Characters

OWNER—Very pleasant and aggressive about the merchandise of his trade.

JOHN (or Jo Anne)—A Christian shopper.

SANDY—A non-Christian shopper. (Could be either male or female.)

Setting

A store with counter and merchandise. Make this as simple or elaborate as you wish.

Lights up on the Owner standing behind the counter, primping his products. John enters, looks around inquisitively.

OWNER   Good afternoon! May I be of some assistance?

JOHN   Yes, thank you. I was looking for something to decorate my house that would bring out the true spirit of Christmas.

OWNER   Why of course! We have plenty of Xmas decorations

---

that are right for you.

JOHN   You mean *Christmas*, right?

OWNER   Whatever. How about this? A miniature plastic X—ah, I mean *Christmas* tree with flashy lights, great colors and a really "in" assortment of ornaments ranging from "Frostymen" to "Glowing Rudolphs." And—there's a cute little music box hidden in the tree that plays "Santa Claus Is Coming to Town."

JOHN   That's not quite what I had in mind. I want something that symbolizes what Christmas really means.

OWNER   Of course, of course! We have this wonderful poster of Bo Derek [or current popular beauty] dressed as Mrs. Claus.

JOHN   (Stares at poster with amazement) Wouldn't she catch cold dressed like that in the North Pole?

OWNER   Cute. Real cute. Would you prefer a Miss Piggy stocking with Kermit snowflakes falling around her? She's well-dressed.

JOHN   (Getting frustrated) No, no—I mean something that has to do with Jesus Christ! His birth! God's great plan!

OWNER   But that's so . . . so traditional. It's boring. This is the 20th century! You gotta get with it! Why, Frosty, Rudolph and the Grinch—that's what Christmas is all about.

JOHN   Ah . . . so that's how the Grinch stole Christmas.

(Sandy enters)

OWNER   (Frustrated) Here. How about a hanging angel? That's religious.

JOHN   (Looking at the angel) Yeah, but wearing designer jeans?

SANDY   Are those in? The Jordache Angel!

JOHN   Oh, brother.

OWNER   Yes! And we also have the Calvin Snowman!

JOHN   Wait a minute, wait a minute. What happened to normal angels, nativity scenes and real Christmas trees?

OWNER See, that's what Christmas is all about—bright, new, fashionable decorations. Not some old drabby shed with smelly animals in it.

JOHN That's exactly why Christmas is so special!

SANDY Smelly donkeys make Christmas special?

JOHN No. The fact that God would have his own Son born in those conditions.

OWNER Wait a minute. Why should God—you know, God, all powerful, Mr. Wonderful God—have his Son born in the dumps? You really can't believe that.

JOHN I'd rather believe in that than a snowman that melts or jeans that go out of style. All of this will be gone in another year.

SANDY Boy, you sure know how to ruin the Christmas spirit.

JOHN Ruin it?

SANDY Yeah, telling us that Frosty melts and that all this stuff will go away.

OWNER (Trying to reassure Sandy) There, there. (To John) See what you've done! (To Sandy) Here, this recording of AC/DC's "Sleigh Ride to Hades" ought to cheer you up.

JOHN Yeah, I heard that was a really hot hit.

SANDY I'm too depressed now. What's Christmas without Frosty or designer jeans?

JOHN What it's supposed to be.

OWNER No, ah . . . (Desperately) Izod Lacoste candy canes is what it's all about!

JOHN AND SANDY Huh?!?

OWNER Yeah—see the red and white stripes on the alligator? And the tail is hooked so you can hang it on the tree.

SANDY (To John) Maybe you're right. A preppy candy cane is a bit much.

(Sandy and John move to exit)

OWNER   Wait! Aren't you interested in any of these Christmas decorations?

JOHN   (Right before he exits) You mean Xmas, right?

(John and Sandy exit)

OWNER   Maybe I should try some of the new Bethlehem Super Heroes action figures.

BLACKOUT (Curtain)

Discussion Questions

1. Is this sketch an exaggeration of true life, or do you think it's an accurate representation of attitudes about Christmas? In what ways do you think it's exaggerated? In what ways is it accurate?

2. Do you believe Christmas is too commercialized and "de-Christianized"? If so, what do you think believers can do to battle this commercialism?

3. What does Christmas mean to you personally? (No pat answers, please.) What does it represent to you spiritually? socially? emotionally? intellectually?

4. How can you make Christmas especially meaningful this year? How about getting the youth group to sing to nursing home residents? collect canned goods for the needy? organize a Christmas party for younger Sunday school children? Come up with a list of ideas, and then do them.

Sketch 9

The Party

(Thanks to Jeremiah People for this one.)

I n this sketch we go to a party and meet a young man who is more interested in picking up a young lady than being sensitive to her real needs.

Characters

KATHY—An attractive, fairly shy girl who is concealing a lot of personal hurt.

CHUCK—An obnoxious "mover" who is sensitive only to his personal needs and desires. He considers himself quite witty and clever and laughs a lot at his own lines (though he should be overplayed to the point of being humorous and not sickening).

JIM—A friend of Chuck's from church.

Setting

A party as represented by a couple of chairs center stage for Kathy and, ultimately, Chuck. Extras would be useful for mingling.

Lights up on Kathy who is sitting on a chair. Chuck enters.

CHUCK   Excuse me! (He smiles as Kathy turns and looks at him somewhat sheepishly) Hi! Is that seat taken? (Pointing to the empty seat beside her)

KATHY Uh, no.

CHUCK (Sliding like a snake into it) It is now! (He sits there with a big grin, checking her out) I'm Chuck.

KATHY (Hesitantly) I'm Kathy.

CHUCK (With a coy smile) You certainly are! Well say, you're kind of new to this area, aren't you?

KATHY We just moved here.

CHUCK We?

KATHY Yeah, my folks and I . . . I'm single.

CHUCK Oh really! Well, uh, who'd you come to the party with?

KATHY I came with Pam (Looking around), but I don't see her anywhere.

CHUCK Oh, don't worry about Pam . . . she's a real swinger. Yeah, good old Pam. We call her "hinges," 'cause she's something to "a-door!" (Laughing) Get the pun . . . hinges . . . a-door . . . (Laughing dies off quickly with no response) Well, say, uh, what do you do besides just sit there and look good?

KATHY I work at the telephone company.

CHUCK Oh really . . . well, that doesn't surprise me 'cause I know you really "ring my chimes." (Laughs at his cleverness)

KATHY What do you do?

CHUCK (Laughter quickly stops) Uh, uh . . . I'm into publications.

KATHY What area?

CHUCK Huh? Oh, I, uh . . . I work in a (Under his breath) religious (Back to normal volume) bookstore. (Quickly) Say, you know, you strike me as a girl with a lot of diversified interests. I mean, I'm a *guy* with a lot of diversified interests! That's right . . . I like to do *all* kinds of things . . . especially sports. I mean, I like to hike, camp and ski. I play football, soccer, hockey . . .

wrestling. Yes-sir-ee, I love it all, as long as it involves a little, uh, "*physical* activity." (Smiling—anxiously awaiting a response)

KATHY   Well, I like literature.

CHUCK   (Smile disappears) Uh, oh yeah, me too! Nothing better than a good book, I always say! Out there hiking, camping, skiing, out on the old basketball court . . . I always got a book. (Smiling and chuckling)

KATHY   My *favorite* is poetry.

CHUCK   (Smile again freezes, then disappears with kind of a sick look) Poetry? Poetry . . . oh yeah, one of my favorites, poetry . . . uh . . . (Thoughtfully trying to remember a poem) . . . okay.

"Little fly upon the wall
Ain't you got no clothes at all?
Ain't you got no woolen shirt?
Ain't you got no pretty skirt?
Little fly aren't you cold?"

(Laughs cleverly) That's a little "free verse." (Laughs) Speaking of free, what are you doing after the party, huh?

KATHY   (Nervously)   Oh, well, I really have to do . . . (She starts to move as if to leave)

CHUCK   (Grabbing her arm) Oh, no, no, no. I mean (Singing) we've only just begun! (He chuckles) I kinda like music, too.

KATHY   (Looking around sheepishly, asking for help) Pam!?

CHUCK   (Looking as if he's noticed something to her right) Say, uh, I don't suppose you'd mind if I had a peanut, would you?

KATHY   (Pausing) No. No, go right ahead.

CHUCK   Fine. (Instead of reaching in front of her, he lifts his *right* arm, puts it *around* her, reaches down and grabs an imaginary peanut. He then puts his *left* arm in *front* of her, drops the peanut from the right to his left hand, and pops the peanut in his mouth. With a smile, he snuggles in closer to her with his right arm still around her. After looking around a bit, he turns toward her, getting a whiff of her perfume. As he moves to get a closer sniff, overplaying the sniffs, a coy smile comes across his face) Say, what's that *great* smell?

KATHY   "Taboo."

CHUCK   Let's hope not! (Once again he chuckles at himself and comments on how clever he is)

(A friend, Jim, briskly enters from stage left and crosses behind Chuck and Kathy. As he does, he notices Chuck and walks over to him)

JIM   Hey, Chuck! How ya doin'? I didn't know you were going to be at this party. (Chuck sees who is speaking and immediately begins to get noticeably uneasy) Hey, I'm glad I ran into you. You know you left your coat over at Bible study the other night. I've got it at my house if you want to pick it up. Incidentally, I really appreciate what you shared the other night about what the Lord has been doing in your life. It really helped me. I gotta run . . . take it easy. (Jim exits)

KATHY   Did he say "Bible study"?

CHUCK   (By now extremely uncomfortable) Uh . . . uh . . . right. I mean . . . you know how I love literature! (Laughing nervously)

KATHY   (Thoughtfully) I knew someone like that once. He said he was a Christian. (Pausing) He seemed so . . . caring. I sure wish I had someone like that to talk to now. (Pausing, then speaking introspectively, almost trancelike) You see, it's . . . uh . . . it's my parents. They are . . . uh . . . getting a divorce. I love them both so much. (Chuck's uneasiness and guilt increase) It's so hard for me to understand and to live with the thought that my *family* is breaking up. I just don't know what to do or where to turn. I was hoping I would find someone here to talk to . . . someone to offer a little help or maybe even a little . . . encouragement. (Looking at Chuck) But I guess that's not the case here. (Pauses as guilt covers Chuck's face) I've got to go. (With tears in her eyes, she quickly stands and leaves. Chuck makes a move to stop her, but it's too late)

CHUCK   Wait a minute, I . . . (He slowly looks back toward audience in guilt and despair as scripture is read . . . read Matthew 5:13-16)

BLACKOUT (Curtain)

Discussion Questions

1. More than anything, this sketch deals with insensitivity, hypocrisy and—to an extent—Chuck's inability to put into practice certain Christian principles. Have you ever been in a situation where you were insensitive to someone else's feelings—not behaving or responding in the way you knew you should? What did you learn from that experience? How did it help you in similar encounters later?

2. We often find ourselves in situations at school or work where we do the exact opposite of what we know we should do. This was accented in the sketch when Jim thanks Chuck for what he shared in the Bible study. Have you ever found yourself in an environment where you were behaving differently than you knew you should? Why did you behave that way? What was the outcome?

3. Do you know anyone like Chuck? How do you respond to him or her? Is there anything you can do to help him or her, if it's your place to do so? What should you do?

Sketch 10

The Reconciliation

In this sketch two church members (could be either male or female) meet to work out their problems—whatever the problems may be.

Characters

PORTER—The accused.
FREDERICKS—The accuser.

Setting

It could be anywhere. Two chairs.

Lights up as Porter and Fredericks enter silently. They sit down. There is a moment of awkward silence.

PORTER	Well?
FREDERICKS	Well what?
PORTER	You wanted to see me. Here I am.
FREDERICKS	Yes . . . well, the Bible says that if we have a grievance with one another, then we should go to the person privately and discuss it. That's why I'm here.
PORTER	A grievance? You have a grievance with me?

FREDERICKS	(Stands, paces) Yes. It's fairly well known that you hate me.
PORTER	Hate is a pretty strong word. We've had our disagreements in the past but—
FREDERICKS	You're saying I'm disagreeable?
PORTER	Not at all.
FREDERICKS	But I am disagreeable. Everyone knows it. I know it.
PORTER	Disagreeable isn't exactly what comes to mind.
FREDERICKS	You're calling me a liar?
PORTER	No, I'm not calling you that.
FREDERICKS	Then what are you calling me?
PORTER	I'm not calling you anything.
FREDERICKS	I'm a nobody, is that what you're saying?
PORTER	(Confused) Yes . . . no . . . I don't know what I'm saying.
FREDERICKS	My point exactly. You never know what you're saying.
PORTER	But I do! At least I did until we started this conversation.
FREDERICKS	Implying that I'm confusing the issue.
PORTER	I'm not implying anything.
FREDERICKS	You're saying it outright.
PORTER	What?
FREDERICKS	What you just said.
PORTER	What did I just say?
FREDERICKS	Don't be coy with me. We should be able to discuss this man to man [Or, "like two intelligent women"].
PORTER	We're one short.
FREDERICKS	Aha! Now you're being insulting.

PORTER	I'm sorry. I couldn't resist.
FREDERICKS	It's too late to apologize. The damage is done.
PORTER	What damage? I haven't been able to figure out what you're talking about.
FREDERICKS	We've done enough talking. Now is the time for action.
PORTER	What kind of action? What are you going to do?
FREDERICKS	More than *you've* done.
PORTER	Done about what? What was I supposed to do?
FREDERICKS	Well, if you don't know, how should I?
PORTER	I guess you wouldn't.
FREDERICKS	Right. (Pauses, confused) So . . . ah . . . do you forgive me or what?
PORTER	Sure. I guess so.
FREDERICKS	What a relief. Boy, those scriptural principles really do work, don't they?
PORTER	They're what I live by.

BLACKOUT (Curtain)

Discussion Questions

1. Early in the sketch, Fredericks states, ". . . the Bible says that if we have a grievance with one another then we should go to the person privately and discuss it." Where in the Bible does it tell us to do that? What exactly does it say to do? (Read Matthew 6:12, 15; 18:35; Luke 6:37; Galatians 6:1-5; Ephesians 4:25-27, 29, 31-32.) Did Fredericks and Porter do as the Bible commands?

2. Think of a recent conflict you've had with a friend, family member, teacher or other person. Have you worked out the conflict with him or her? Why or why not? According to the Bible, what should you do if you were the person who was offended? What should you do if the fault is truly yours? Make a point to resolve the conflict during this next week.

Sketch 11

Protection

In this sketch a government agent gives some surprising news to a "conservative" Christian.

Characters

ZUCKER—A "conservative" Christian.

FLOYD JACKLE—A government agent. Straightforward, almost monotone (similar to Jack Webb in the old television series *Dragnet*).

Setting

Zucker's living room. Two chairs are enough. More elaboration is up to you.

Lights up on Zucker's living room. Jackle enters—looking official wearing a suit, overcoat, dark sunglasses, and carrying a clipboard. Zucker follows holding a small business card.

ZUCKER   You're Floyd Jackle with what government agency?

JACKLE   The Office of Wildlife Protection. Or, the Wildlife Protection Office. Mind if we sit down?

ZUCKER   No, go right ahead. (They both sit down) If you're looking for a contribution, I'm not really int—

JACKLE   No, no, no. That's not why I'm here at all.

ZUCKER   Then what can I do for you? I'm not a hunter.

JACKLE   I just need to double-check my information. You're Ralph (Looks at clipboard) Ralph D. Zucker. Correct?

ZUCKER   Yes.

JACKLE   And you believe that the Bible is the inspired, inerrant Word of God?

ZUCKER   Yes.

JACKLE   And Jesus Christ was born of a virgin, performed literal miracles, raised people from the dead, was crucified for your sins and himself rose from the dead three days later?

ZUCKER   Yes. He is God incarnate.

JACKLE   "God incarnate." Yes, I'll add that.

ZUCKER   What is this?

JACKLE   You believe in the Genesis account of creation?

ZUCKER   Yes.

JACKLE   And Jesus is the only way to get to heaven—not one of many different ways?

ZUCKER   Right.

JACKLE   A person cannot get to heaven by good works?

ZUCKER   No, a person cannot.

JACKLE   Hell is a literal place of punishment for those who do not accept Christ?

ZUCKER   It is.

JACKLE   Heaven and eternal life await believers after death? Literally?

ZUCKER   Literally, yes.

JACKLE   And Jesus Christ will return literally and physically to earth one day?

ZUCKER   He will.

JACKLE   (Stands) You don't smoke, drink, chew or go with women who do, and never attend movies with more than a "G" rating?

ZUCKER   No, I don't.

JACKLE   Well, sir, under Ordinance 215701264-51784, you are entitled to protection as an endangered species because of the rarity of your habitat and lifestyle. If you ever feel endangered, give me a call. Congratulations. Good day, sir. (He exits quickly)

ZUCKER   (Still sitting, dumbfounded, looks at the card with disbelief, long pause) Gee, I knew that living right would pay off big someday.

BLACKOUT (Curtain)

Discussion Questions

1. Examine each point of belief as confirmed by Zucker to Jackle. How closely do your beliefs align with Mr. Zucker's? In what ways are your beliefs similar? different?

2. How would you define such a term as "conservative" Christian? Do you consider yourself a conservative Christian? If not, how would you label yourself? How do you think conservative Christians are viewed by your church? by your friends? by your family? by the general public?

3. Do you think conservative Christians, like Zucker, are "endangered," or more difficult to find? Why or why not?

Sketch 12

Long Time No See

In this sketch two "friends" meet on the street for a pleasant conversation—with unpleasant thoughts behind it.

Characters

JIM—An overconfident overachiever.
JERRY—The guy who always finishes second—and isn't real happy about it.

Setting

Could take place on a street or anywhere informal. Bare stage.

Lights up as Jim and Jerry enter from opposite sides of the stage.

JIM   Jerry! Long time no see! Workin' in the same company, you'd think we'd run into each other more often.

JERRY   Yeah, well that big promotion you got put you in a different part of the office. Say, I don't know if I ever took the time to say it, but . . . congratulations!

JIM   (Confidently smiling) Well, thanks!

JERRY   You deserved it! (Aside) This guy has got an ego the size of a warehouse. He gets one little promotion and he thinks he's Lee Iacocca! (End aside)

JIM Well, it just goes to show you what a little hard work and perseverance will do.

JERRY (Smiling) Right!

JIM (Aside) This clown has been bad-mouthing me behind my back ever since I got this promotion. He's just ticked he didn't get it. (End aside) So, how are things with Marge and the kids? I hear she's having a hard time with the pregnancy.

JERRY Pregnancy? Oh, you mean Jonathan . . . he just turned 3.

JIM Really! Boy, time flies . . . it seems like yesterday! (Aside) Okay, so I'm not so good with time. At least I asked. (End aside) I understand your mom's been a little under the weather. How's she doing?

JERRY Oh, she's doing better . . . much better, thanks! (Aside) Now what does this guy care about my family? His idea of showing concern is sending a Hallmark card. (End aside)

JIM Good! Say, did she get that card I sent?

JERRY You bet. Thanks a lot!

JIM Oh, it was nothing.

JERRY (Aside) That's the understatement of the year. (End aside)

JIM I hope she enjoyed it.

JERRY She loved it.

JIM Great! (Aside) This guy is about as grateful to me as a snail is to salt. (End aside) Things must be pretty tight financially for you at home with three kids and your mother living with you.

JERRY Yeah, but we'll make it somehow.

JIM (Smiling) Good. (Aside) 'Cause he ain't gonna get a red cent outta me! (End aside)

JERRY Say, I thought I saw you driving your old Camaro around the other day. You finally got it fixed after our little "fender bender" accident in the parking lot.

JIM   Sure did! (Aside) Fender bender! Ol' Daryl Demolition
          here rear ended me and about turned my Camaro into
          a Chevette! I should have sued him for everything he
          had . . . including his bad attitude! (End aside) It's run-
          ning like a charm!

JERRY   Great! (Aside) You know, to this day he and his wife are
          convinced it was my fault. The fact is, he backed right
          into me, and then they backed right out of our lives.
          (End aside) Say, whatever happened to that group you
          used to lead?

JIM   (Nervously) Group? What group? (Aside) If he brings up
          the Bible study, I'll die of embarrassment. (End aside)

JERRY   I don't know. That small group you had going.

JIM   Small group. I don't . . .

JERRY   Come on, you remember. You and Louise were always
          after me and Marge to come to your house for a get-
          together. What was it—Amway?

JIM   (As if finally realizing) Oh no, that was a . . . ah . . .
          (Mumbles inaudibly) a Bible study. So Jonathan's 3 years
          old already. Boy, he must be big now. (Aside) Got out of
          that one. (End aside)

JERRY   Yeah, he sure is but I'm sorry, I didn't hear what you
          said about those meetings.

JIM   What meetings?

JERRY   The meetings that you—oh, never mind. I must be think-
          ing of someone else.

JIM   Must be. (Aside) I couldn't invite this guy to our Bible
          study, he'd never fit in. He's not ready for the Gospel
          yet, anyway. Besides, all he's ever given me is grief. (End
          aside) Good seeing you again.

JERRY   Right. Good seeing you. (Aside) This guy could give a fly-
          ing rip about me or my family. In his mind I'm just
          another rung to step on while climbing the corporate
          ladder. (End aside) Give us a call if you get the chance.
          (Aside) But don't push yourself. (End aside)

JIM   Will do! (Aside) But don't wait by the phone. (End aside)

JIM   (Together as an aside as they exit) Creep. (End aside)
AND
JERRY

BLACKOUT (Curtain)

Discussion Questions

1. These two men were obviously friends at one time. What happened to their relationship? How could the deterioration of their relationship have been avoided? What would it take to mend their relationship?

2. How do you think the problems in Jim and Jerry's relationship might also affect their relationships with God?

3. What can you learn from this sketch? Are there any relationships in your life similar to the one we see here? What should you do about them?

4. How can you avoid future misunderstandings with friends? List ways you can keep honesty, openness and forgiveness in all of your relationships.

Sketch 13

The Bible Study

In this sketch we see the birth, development and dissolution of a Bible study group.

Characters

NARRATOR
CHUCK—The group leader. Very enthusiastic.
BOB—Dogmatic.
FRED—Equally dogmatic.
DON—A fairly laid-back (if not scandalous) accountant.
LOUISE—An extremely withdrawn woman.
BETTY—A modern woman.
ELAINE—A regular kind of gal.

Setting

Chuck's living room. A small circle of chairs.

Several people—Chuck, Bob, Fred, Don, Louise, Betty and Elaine—along with a few extras, enter and sit down. The Bible study leader, Chuck, has a guitar in hand. They freeze in a seated position until the Narrator has spoken.

NARRATOR   One of the great ministries of our church is the Bible study group. It can be an opportunity for people of diverse backgrounds to come together in unity, study their Bibles, and share in mutual fellowship and development as believers. It can be the one night of the week that serves to energize and motivate. It can be a place to open up hearts—to be vulnerable, to question, to doubt, to reaffirm. It can be all these things.

It *can* be.

Let's drop in on Chuck, our novice group leader, and one particular Bible study group as it meets for the first time.

(Beat) Any resemblance between the Bible study you are about to see and those currently in existence is a crying shame.

(With that said, the Narrator turns and exits. Chuck immediately begins strumming away at the guitar—almost frantically—with barely distinguishable chords. He sings a popular praise chorus—with equal energy. Everyone else sits and looks at him blankly)

CHUCK   Okay! One more time on that chorus!

(He sings a portion of the song again—still no one joining in—the same blank looks—he comes to a big finish and, obviously out of breath, laughs and puts the guitar aside)

CHUCK   Boy, don't you just love those praise choruses?

(Blank looks)

CHUCK   Yeah, well, they sure minister to me. Welcome to our very first growth group. Glad you're all here. I am, of course, anticipating an incredible time to study our Bibles and cultivate personal growth in Christ and discover the kinds of sharing that'll build friendships and support each other through prayer and encouragement.

BOB   (Spoken sternly, challenging) Do you believe in a pre-trib, mid-trib, or post-trib rapture?

CHUCK   Huh?

BOB   Pre-, mid-, or post-trib rapture?

CHUCK   Well . . . ah . . . I'll take it any way I can get it. (Laughs) Okay. Hey. Just kidding. I think there's a different Bible study group dealing with those questions. This is the study of the book of Leviticus— and an exciting book it is, too—with tons of laws to draw practical application from. Now the way I see us doing this is to first sing like we just did, then maybe a time for prayer requests and personal intimate encounters, then the Bible study and Louise— raise your hand, Louise, just in case we don't have all the names down yet.

(Blank looks. Louise—the wallflower—hangs her head shyly and raises her hand ever so slightly)

CHUCK   Louise is providing the food and refreshments tonight. What did you bring, Louise?

LOUISE   (Almost inaudibly) Twinkies and Gatorade.

CHUCK   Oh, don't be so shy, Louise. We're one big open family here—right, gang?

(Blank looks)

CHUCK   Of course we are. Now, what did you say you brought, Louise?

LOUISE   (Louder but still soft) Twinkies and Gatorade.

CHUCK   Twinkies and Gatorade. (Tries to subdue his nausea) Yeah, right, and we'll be looking forward to that a little later in the evening. What do you say we get into some prayer requests and personal share time?

(Blank looks)

BOB   Do you believe in immediate, mediate or the Augustine viewpoint on the imputation of sin?

CHUCK   Huh?

BOB   Do you believe . . . ?

CHUCK   Why don't we save questions for the Bible study portion of the evening? Does anybody have anything they want to share personally at this time?

(Blank looks)

CHUCK What has the Lord done in your life? Anything?

(Blank looks)

CHUCK Has he taught you anything recently?

(Blank looks)

CHUCK Are there any prayer requests?

(Blank looks)

CHUCK Does anybody know what time it is?

(Blank looks)

BOB (Looking at watch) It is 8:05.

CHUCK Great. Fred, why don't you dismiss us with prayer?

(They freeze in place as the Narrator enters again)

NARRATOR It's true. The first meeting is often a little . . . uncomfortable. But let's look at the same Bible study about a month later. Notice the intensity, the zeal to discuss . . .

(The group unfreezes in the midst of an argument as the Narrator exits)

BOB But the theological ramifications are staggering if what you say is true! The whole foundation of Christianity would shift!

FRED You're making a big deal out of nothing! I truly believe that God—in his love and mercy—wouldn't penalize the innocent like that! It would suggest that he is not who he claims he is!

BOB No, no, no! It reinforces who he says he is!

CHUCK (Trying to get control) Guys . . .

FRED Show me scripture on that!

CHUCK Okay, guys! Hold on.

BOB	Show me scripture supporting your conclusions . . .
CHUCK	Whoa! We've gotten a little off the track here. Now, I think we should just go ahead and *pray* for Louise's parakeet and let God do as he will. No harm in trying. (Beat) But I'm not sure that the bird's illness is indicative of sin in Louise's life. Right, Louise?
LOUISE	Oh, I hope not. (Questioning herself) Well, I don't think so. (Resolved) Of course not. (Afraid that it is) Oh, that poor bird.
CHUCK	Okay. Fine. (Trying to be encouraging) But, hey, I appreciate you guys getting involved like that. It's good to have somebody but me talking.
BOB	Amen.
CHUCK	But, I'll tell you what—let's save the theological debate for after prayer time. Okay? Now, are there any other prayer requests?

(Blank looks)

CHUCK	Would someone like to lead us, then?

(Blank looks)

CHUCK	Aw, come on, guys. Surely somebody wants to pray.

(Louise sheepishly raises her hand)

CHUCK	(Encouraged) There you go. Good for you, Louise.
LOUISE	I don't want to pray. I was just wondering if I could retract the prayer request for my parakeet? It really *might* be sin in my life.
CHUCK	But . . . it's our only prayer request. We won't have anything to pray for if you retract it.
LOUISE	Well . . . go ahead, then. If anything happens, I'll just buy another one. They're not hard to get.
CHUCK	Thanks. I guess I'll lead.

(Bowing their heads, they freeze as the Narrator enters)

NARRATOR   The same Bible study. The eighth week. As time has moved on, our group has become unified in spirit and emotion—reaching the pinnacle of everything this group could hope to be. Everyone begins to share willingly during the course of the evening—sometimes leaving the members drained emotionally when things wind down.

(Narrator exits. The group unfreezes and looks somewhat drained emotionally. There is a tell-tale quiet about them. Everyone is smiling pleasantly—looking one to another. One or two reach over and place their hands on the shoulder or hand of the person next to them—or other gestures of affection)

CHUCK   What a night it's been, huh? Boy . . . I never would have expected the Levitical laws on leprosy to bring out so much in us.

(There are a few chuckles)

CHUCK   I don't know about you, but I'm drained. Louise, thank you for sharing that experience with us. I think we all now have a greater understanding of what it's like to be married six times.

LOUISE   Seven.

CHUCK   Seven. That's right. What pain, what suffering!

LOUISE   I've suffered, too.

CHUCK   I'm sure you have. Wow. You know, when we started this group, I figured I'd need a crowbar to get a word out of you. Any of you. But, boy, when you open up, you really open up. And Betty, thanks for showing us the snapshots of your trip to Illinois.

BETTY   Texas.

CHUCK   Right. Those shots of your cousins branding cattle were . . . well, I can't even think of the word. (Don gestures that he wants to speak) Go ahead, Don.

DON   I don't know about you guys but . . . I feel like something special has happened between us tonight. I feel closer to you guys now than I have to anyone in my whole life. I know I confessed some things tonight that I've never told anyone before. And because of that, I feel like God has forgiven me for the wrongs I've done and maybe . . . maybe I can forgive myself, too. Maybe I can even give back the half-a-million I embezzled from my company.

(Everyone nods affirmatively)

CHUCK	I'm sure you can, Don. (To Bob) And you'll be taking over as treasurer next week, right, Bob? (To Don) Nothing personal, of course.
DON	That's fine.
CHUCK	And, hey, I'm glad you're here, Don. I thank God for you. For all of you. (Pause) Well . . . I guess we should call it a night. What time is it, anyway?
FRED	Almost midnight.
CHUCK	(Chuckles) We ran a little overtime.
BETTY	Only two-and-a-half hours.
CHUCK	Should we take up a collection for your baby sitter?
BETTY	(Amused) It might help.
DON	I'll pass the hat around in a minute.
CHUCK	Ah, Bob . . . why don't you take over as treasurer *this* week? (After a thoughtful pause) . . . I just want to say that this is the kind of night that makes me glad I'm doing this Bible study. Even the pistachio and raisin pie was exceptionally interesting, Louise. (Pauses) Let's close with a word of prayer . . .

(They bow their heads and freeze in place as the Narrator enters)

NARRATOR	The twelfth week. Our Bible study members have gone one step beyond their unity of purpose to complete comfort with each other . . . and a thoroughly casual attitude about why they're meeting.

(As the Narrator exits, the group comes up from prayer. Everyone gets comfortable, relaxed)

CHUCK   Amen. Okay, let's open up to Leviticus . . .

(Movement is slow, very casual)

FRED   (To Don) I got two tickets to the Dodgers Friday
             night. Are you interested? (Even as he speaks, Louise
             leans to Betty and begins a separate conversation)

DON   Friday? I don't think I have anything planned. Let
             me give you a call tomorrow.

LOUISE   My sister-in-law has a pair of shoes just like yours.

BETTY   She does?

LOUISE   I think hers might be a little lighter color, though.

BETTY   I saw those. I got these because they match a dress
             I bought at Garfinkel's.

CHUCK   Leviticus, folks.

ELAINE   (Joining in the conversation with Betty and Louise)
             Do you like the lower heels or the higher ones?

BETTY   I like the lower heels.

BOB	(To Fred) I was reading last week that the work on the freeway has hit another budget snag. It takes me almost an hour to get to work now.	LOUISE	My husband likes the higher heels.
		BETTY	Your husband wears high heels?
			(They laugh)
CHUCK	Folks?	LOUISE	Not with his legs.
FRED	I'm not surprised. I've been trying to go in to work earlier but the traffic seems just as bad.		(They laugh again)

DON	My office is considering a swing-shift schedule.	**ELAINE**	I need lower heels for work. I don't think I could make it a full day with the high heels.
BOB	A lot of offices are going to that.		
DON	I wouldn't mind it. I get tired sitting in rush hour.	**BETTY**	(Proudly) I got promoted day before yesterday.
FRED	I read the paper.	**LOUISE**	You did? That's great!

(Chuck picks up the guitar and destroys another praise chorus with his playing and singing. They stop, look at him)

CHUCK   (Puts guitar down) I thought that would get your attention. (Gestures to Bible) Leviticus? Third book of the Bible? Please?

BOB   (Slowly getting his Bible) Did you know that the Hebrew Bible has a different number of books in it than ours? They combine I and 2 Kings, 1 and 2 Chronicles, 1 and 2 Samuel . . .

DON   I guess sequels weren't as important to them as they are to us.

FRED   I heard a rumor that Sylvester Stallone is going to do another *Rocky* movie.

BOB   Who could be left for him to fight?

DON   E.T.

BETTY   Did you see *E.T.*?

ELAINE   Who hasn't?

BETTY   I thought it was wonderful.

ELAINE   Who didn't?

(They begin talking about movies animately as Chuck turns sideways on his chair and rests his head on his hand resignedly)

CHUCK   Familiarity breeds distraction.

BOB   I thought it was "contempt."

CHUCK   That's next.

(They freeze. The Narrator enters again. As he does, everyone except Chuck and Bob exits)

NARRATOR   And, finally . . . the last week of the Bible study.

(Narrator exits. Chuck and Bob unfreeze and look at each other)

CHUCK   Well, what do you think? Should we start or wait a few minutes longer?

BOB   It's almost 8:30. We should go ahead and start. I don't think anyone else is coming.

CHUCK   I wonder what happened to everyone? This is our last class. You would have thought they'd make it for this.

BOB   I know Fred said something about being out of town. Betty is in some civic tennis tournament. And I guess you read in the paper about Don.

CHUCK   Yeah . . . (Confounded) You know, he told me he gave the money back.

BOB   I'm sure it was just a misunderstanding. His wife'll have him bailed out tonight.

CHUCK   Good. Okay, let's start. (He reaches to pick up the guitar)

BOB   Ah, Chuck . . . you don't have to do that.

CHUCK   No songs?

BOB   No songs. Frankly, to be quite honest, we've never liked the songs. We've been trying to figure out how to tell you short of giving you money for guitar lessons.

CHUCK   Oh.

BOB   I guess we're just not the musical types.

CHUCK   I guess not. (Looks to the empty room) So this is how it ends. My first shot as group leader. We were supposed to do evaluations tonight.

BOB   Do you want me to do one?

CHUCK   Not really.

BOB   I would if you wanted. I think you've done a great job. This group has meant a lot to me even with its quirks. (Pause) I'm going to miss Louise's surprise snacks.

CHUCK   Me, too. The chocolate chip watermelon was my favorite.

(Long pause)

CHUCK   I haven't had dinner. Do you want to go out and get some pizza?

BOB   Sure.

(They stand, begin to exit)

BOB   By the way? What *do* you believe in? A pre-trib, mid-trib, or post-trib rapture?

CHUCK   I don't know. What's a trib?

(They exit. Narrator enters again)

NARRATOR   And that was the beginning of a beautiful friendship.

(Narrator exits)

BLACKOUT (Curtain)

Discussion Questions

1. Do you think this sketch is reasonably accurate in representing the stages of a Bible study? Why or why not? Does this Bible study remind you of any Bible studies you've been in? If so, how? Did you enjoy that Bible study group? What and how did you gain from it? What would you have improved?

2. Think of the best Bible study group in which you've ever participated. Now think of the worst one. Compare the two. What qualities did the best one have? What problems did the worst one have?

3. Can you relate to any of the characters in this sketch? If so, which ones? How do you relate to them? What advice would you give these characters to improve their Bible study based on what you see in this sketch?

4. How can you apply the lessons learned from this sketch to your youth group Bible studies?

Sketch 14

The Counseling Session

In this sketch a pastor's confidentiality comes under question by an unusual visitor.

Characters

PASTOR STRINGER—A well-meaning minister. Can be male or female.

RICK BRADY (or Rhonda)—The counselee.

Setting

Pastor's office. At least two chairs. Elaborate as much or as little as you wish.

Lights up on Pastor Stringer sitting at his desk (or reading a book in a chair, etc.). Rick Brady enters.

RICK   Pastor? Pastor Stringer?

PASTOR   (Looking up) Yes, sir? What can I do for you?

RICK   (Approaching hesitantly) You don't know me but . . . my name is, um . . . Ralph Jones and . . . well, I was wondering if we could talk.

PASTOR	Of course. Please sit down.
RICK	(Sitting down) I'm not a church-going person, you understand, but I've got a lot on my mind and . . . well, I didn't know who else to talk to.
PASTOR	That's fine, Mr.? I'm sorry, what did you say your name is?
RICK	Bill Smith.
PASTOR	Fine, Mr. Smith. What seems to be bothering you?
RICK	(Looking around to be sure no one is listening) I have a confession I want to make.
PASTOR	I'm not a priest.
RICK	That's all right. This isn't a Catholic confession. But . . . you guys don't divulge confidences, do you? I mean, what I say here is strictly between us, correct? I mean, don't you pastors take some sort of vow to be quiet?
PASTOR	No. But I consider this office and conversations held here to be strictly confidential . . . unless they make for good sermon illustrations. (Rick looks at him blankly) That's supposed to be a joke.
RICK	Oh.
PASTOR	Generally, I adhere to strict rules of confidentiality.
RICK	"Generally." What do you mean "generally"? You got exceptions?
PASTOR	Oh, I suppose if it were something terribly illegal (Chuckles from the absurdity of the thought), or if you killed someone or something like that. I would have to encourage you to turn yourself in or . . . call the police myself.
RICK	Oh. (Slowly stands) Thank you, then.
PASTOR	(Surprised) You're leaving?
RICK	Yes.
PASTOR	(Perplexed) It's . . . that serious?

RICK   What you just said.

PASTOR   Something terribly illegal?

RICK   The other thing.

PASTOR   You're joking.

RICK   Nah. I'm dead serious . . . no pun intended, of course. It's just that I feel very guilty about the whole matter. Oh well, maybe I'll go find a priest. Have a nice day. (He exits)

PASTOR   Hey, wait a minute! (Settles back) What a shame. It would have fit in nicely with my Cain and Abel sermon this week.

BLACKOUT (Curtain)

Discussion Questions

1. How confidential should conversations with the pastor be? Strictly confidential regardless of the circumstances, or partially confidential if the circumstances seem to warrant bringing in outside authorities? Why?

2. Imagine this: A young girl goes to her pastor for counseling. She's a teenager, unmarried, and has recently found out that she's pregnant. She doesn't want her parents to know anything about it because she's trying to decide what to do—even an abortion is possible. If you were her pastor, would you honor her desire to keep this information from her parents, or would you tell them? Why or why not? Come up with other scenarios and discuss how you would handle them.

3. "I consider this office and conversations held here to be strictly confidential . . . unless they make for good sermon illustrations," this pastor says jokingly. How do you feel about pastors using counseling situations as sermon illustrations—even when they use them "anonymously"? Is it right or wrong, good or bad? Why or why not? Does your pastor anonymously use counseling situations as sermon illustrations? If so, how do you feel about it?

4. Has a friend ever told you a problem and asked you not to tell anybody? If so, were you able to maintain confidentiality? Explain. Under what circumstances would you break confidentiality and tell parents or other authorities? Why?

Sketch 15

Luther

In this sketch we meet Martin Luther and hear some of his thoughts. (This sketch is especially appropriate for Reformation Sunday—but applicable any time.)

Characters

NARRATOR

MARTIN LUTHER—Should be played with a contemporary style in manner and speech, while capturing the sincerity and passion of the man.

Setting

A stage that suggests a study. A desk and chair.

Lights up on Narrator.

NARRATOR   This is Reformation Sunday, _____.
It was on October 31st of 1517 that an Augustinian friar by the name of Martin Luther openly challenged the practices and theological foundation of *his* church . . . the holy Church of Rome. (Luther enters, casually dressed in contemporary clothes, removing his sweater as he is seated.) By posting his 95 theses of debate on the door of Castle Church at Wittenberg, Luther began a reform that transcended

its own theology by penetrating the hearts of the common people and setting the foundational course of the Protestant church as we know it today.

Imagine now, Martin Luther visiting us *here* today. Speaking many of the words he himself wrote, yet not dressed in the garb of his day nor with the German dialect with which he spoke . . . just Martin Luther . . . the man.

LUTHER   Oh, pardon me. I was just writing down some thoughts. I must do that quite frequently . . . they tell me I've managed to complete some 60,000 pages *full* of those thoughts. Some might think this is a bit pretentious, but my fellow believers are so hungry to consume what has become a new way of thinking, that I felt it necessary to accommodate *their* desire and satisfy *my own* need to put on paper those matters regarding our loving God which have become so important to me.

In retrospect, I am amazed and humbled at the profound effect my thought and actions had on the church. I never set out to divide the church or destroy the fragile unity of my medieval civilization. To the end, I thought of myself as a faithful restorer of the purity of the universal church . . . a renovator, not an innovator.

Now . . . for those who wish to know about my heritage, let me indulge you. I was born in 1483 in Eisleben . . . a small hamlet in what you now call East Germany. I was the son of a peasant laborer whose hard work enabled me to attend school and eventually graduate at the age of 21 from the University at Erfurt. I had planned to go on and study law, but one overcast day, while walking back to the university, I was actually knocked to the ground by a bolt of lightning. I was convinced that God had intervened and spared me. It was then that I committed my way to him and promised to become a monk.

As with all things in my life, I approached being a monk with fervor and dedication. I would fast for days, extend vigils far beyond what was expected, perform menial and noxious chores, confess every sin I could imagine, then return and confess more again. Yet this brought me no peace, only terror of a judgmental God I could not appease. For *10* years I read the Bible again and again. It was as if the Bible was a tree and I had shaken every branch because I wanted to know what it was and what it meant. Yet I was still tormented by my conscience, fearing the righteous wrath of God . . . until I began to meditate on the Apostle Paul's epistle to the Romans. I read Romans 1:17 over and over . . . "For therein is the righteousness of God revealed . . . the just shall live by *faith*." The whole of scripture revealed a different countenance to me. God's mercy is *freely* given . . . the flesh must die that the spirit might live. When we are lowest, he will reach down and raise us through his grace. Not by payment of alms or performing good works, but through faith alone. This passage in Romans opened for me the gates of paradise. I felt I was born again. I knew, too, that this pivotal truth of God's Word held within it the ability to free humanity from the bondage of guilt *and* from the unscriptural edicts imposed by the church. It was this all-encompassing injustice that impelled me to post my 95 theses of debate on the door at Wittenberg. The consequences that followed are well-known. I was excommunicated and eventually asked to deny the treatises which I put forth. But I could not and *would* not recant.

The years that followed were filled with opportunities to instruct and expound on topics heretofore untouched or repressed by the church. Issues like marriage and the priesthood. To *me* it only seemed right and a part of God's plan to be wed. I, myself, married at age 42 and, in so doing, found marriage to be a delight . . . love and joy without ceasing. We bore a child, Magdalena. She was my joy, a bright and shining star in both our lives. Just after her 14th birthday, she contracted a brief and unknown illness. The memory that day of gently holding her in my arms as she died has become a constant poignant reminder of our loving Father's sovereignty.

I also took great joy in writing hymns and in making congregational singing a regular part of worship. You see, I found great inspiration, entertainment and solace in music, and quite frankly felt that the devil did not stay where there was music. In the span of my years I wrote 37 hymns, probably the most recognized of which is taken from Psalm 46— "A Mighty Fortress Is Our God."

But, truly, all of these things pale in comparison to the joy I felt in being able to translate and print the Bible, getting it into the hands of the common people. You see, when all the trappings of life are stripped away, we must recognize that the Bible is to be our vineyard and it is *there* we should all labor and toil. In *all* these things which I did, God's Word was at the core . . . God's holy, unimpeachable Word. Stay true to God's Word. Live it. Preach it. Teach it in the bosom of your families and in the vastness of public assembly, and, if you believe it with all your heart, . . . then sing it!

(Luther then leads the audience in singing "A Mighty Fortress Is Our God")

Discussion Questions

1. How much do you know about Martin Luther? Did you learn anything in the sketch that you didn't know before? What impressions do you now have of the man?

2. How do Luther's perceptions about faith and grace align with your own? Are there any differences? If so, what are they? What scriptural support can you find for Luther's views? for your own?

3. In many ways, Luther was considered a "radical" and "heretic" by the church in his time and remained in danger of being put to death for his beliefs. Would you be as willing to stand up for your own beliefs? Explain. In what ways do your beliefs make you an "outsider" to others at school? work? or even within your church?

The Pastors' Union

In this sketch we meet a group of pastors trying to form a union that will look out for their best interests.

Characters

PASTOR SMITH—The newcomer to this scheme.

PASTOR DANIELS—The primary spokesperson. He's pastor of Church of the Suburbia.

PASTOR WESSON—A staunch believer in the union. Tough, urban approach. He's pastor of Metropolitan Church.

PASTOR HOPPER—She's the pastor from the First Church of the Liberated Saints. She's polite yet very firm and dogmatic about the union.

Setting

Pastor Smith's office. Four chairs will do the job but you can elaborate more if you want.

Lights up on Pastor Smith's office. Everyone enters (Pastor Smith is speaking as they do), finds a chair and sits down.

SMITH   Sorry I don't have a larger office but—it's all I have.

DANIELS   Hopefully this meeting will take care of that.

SMITH   Yes—about that—you have me puzzled. On the phone you said . . . well, what did you say?

DANIELS   Let me get some amenities out of the way first. (Gestures to appropriate people) This is Pastor Wesson from Metropolitan Church. This is Pastor Hopper from First Church of the Liberated Saints. And I am, of course, Pastor Daniels from Church of the Suburbia.

SMITH   Nice to meet you. Now, what's this all about?

DANIELS   We represent a new coalition to form a union.

SMITH   A union? What kind of union?

DANIELS   A pastors' union.

SMITH   A pastors' union?

HOPPER   Yes, we feel it's time that pastors everywhere have unified backing—to ensure the same basic benefits as workers in any other field or vocation.

SMITH   I don't get it. What would this union do?

WESSON   What every union does! Fight for our rights!

SMITH   But I'm a pastor. I'm not supposed to have any rights.

WESSON   A popular misconception. It's time for a change. Brother Daniels?

DANIELS   (Pulling paper from coat pocket) Here's what we're after . . . as just a sample, of course. (Begins reading) The union would guarantee complete health and dental programs.

SMITH   Health and dental?

WESSON   Who wants a pastor with yellow teeth? Your congregation doesn't.

SMITH   My wife certainly doesn't.

HOPPER   How often have you been counseling someone and been aware of your breath? A dental program is a necessity for you to be effective as a pastor.

DANIELS   The union would also negotiate your salary.

SMITH   Salary? You people get salaries?

WESSON   And not just a salary but a percentage as well.

DANIELS   It's what we call our "Great Commission Plan." You'll get a percentage of the tithes brought in by new members.

SMITH   (Not comprehending) A percentage of the tithes?

WESSON   We're talking incentives, Bill. Do you mind if I call you Bill?

SMITH   Not at all. But my name is John.

WESSON   We'd negotiate your salary twice a year . . .

SMITH   Twice!

WESSON   And that doesn't count cost-of-living raises, an expense account and company—that is, *church*—car.

SMITH   Expense account and car?

DANIELS   American made, of course. We have other unions to think of.

HOPPER   You see, this isn't a low-class union we're talking about. We're in a position to get you two weeks vacation minimum this year, personal days and sick days.

WESSON   And your work week will be 35 hours at full pay.

DANIELS   With time and a half, overtime and double time on Sundays.

SMITH   But Sundays are my busiest days!

DANIELS   (Shrugs matter-of-factly) There you are.

HOPPER   We are also working with various Bible publishing houses for kickbacks.

SMITH   I don't understand. Are you talking about Bibles with the church name on them?

WESSON   We're talking about financial remuneration for endorsements from the pulpit. Use a particular Bible for your sermon, mention the name and publisher, and they'll give you something for the advertising.

DANIELS   As pastor, you have a lot of influence over the buying habits of your congregation.

WESSON   Who knows where it can go from there? Bibles, commentaries, lexicons . . . breakfast cereals!

HOPPER   (Sudden thought) Oh! You forgot to mention the mental health benefits.

DANIELS   Oh, yes. Under your health benefits you'll get insurance against burnout and stress-related health problems. From hospitalization to a sanitarium, if necessary. We thought it was a nice added feature.

SMITH   It is. But I don't plan on going crazy.

HOPPER   Who does? Part of the beauty of this union is that it anticipates the worst.

WESSON   (As if adding to the slogan) But it gives you the best. We're talking guaranteed study and preparation time for sermons, standard appointment hours, only one middle-of-the-night emergency per month . . .

SMITH   How can you guarantee that?

WESSON   (Tough confidence) Hey, we're union. We have our ways.

SMITH   Okay, okay, I'm intrigued by all this. But what if my church refuses to go along with it?

WESSON   (Very tough) Just give us the names of the opposers and we'll take care of it.

(Daniels and Hopper look at Wesson —surprised at his indiscretion)

SMITH   You're joking, of course.

(As Daniels tries to cover for him, Wesson merely shrugs)

DANIELS   Of course. If your church refuses, then you strike.

SMITH   A pastors' strike.

DANIELS   How else?

WESSON   We're talking picket lines, press coverage, the works.

	See how long this church lasts without you as pastor.
SMITH	I'm not sure I want to know.
DANIELS	Are you in? We'd love to have you join us.
SMITH	(Pauses, thinking, then slowly stands—the rest take the hint and do the same) Well . . . I'd really like to think about it awhile.
WESSON	Pray about it, too.
SMITH	Can I? Will prayer be included in the contract?
DANIELS	We can negotiate for it, if you want.
SMITH	Thanks. I'll get back to you. (Smith shakes their hands) I appreciate you coming by.
HOPPER	Our pleasure. (They mutter farewells and exit, leaving Pastor Smith alone to contemplate all they've said)
SMITH	(Looking around at his office—such as it is) I could use a larger office. (He moves across stage in opposite direction as lights fade to blackout)

Discussion Questions

1. Does the idea of a pastors' union seem absurd to you? Why or why not?

2. Pastor Smith states at one point that he is not "supposed to have any rights" because he is a pastor. Do you think that statement is accurate? Why or why not?

3. What does the Bible say about the pastor and his or her responsibilities? (For example, read 1 Timothy 3:1-13; Titus 1:5-9.) What thoughts do you have concerning the work of your pastor? What are your expectations of your pastor? Does he or she fulfill those expectations? Explain. Are your expectations realistic? How do you think your pastor could improve himself or herself as your pastor? How could you improve yourself as a member of the congregation?

4. What should the church's responsibility be toward its pastor—financially and otherwise? To what extent should a church take care of its pastor? Should a church (or church association) cover all of the health areas described in this sketch? Why or why not?

5. Does this sketch provide you with any new thoughts about your pastor and the amount of work he or she does throughout the week—at any hour? Explain. As a youth group, think of ways you can show your appreciation to your pastor. For example, make a huge thank-you banner out of newsprint. Have every youth group member and sponsor sign it; then hang the banner in the pastor's office or church hallway.

Sketch 17

Something About Hagar

In this sketch we meet a couple of Old Testament women waiting for a "church" service to begin.

Characters

DEBORAH—Fairly normal, tries to be sensitive.
ANNA—Stubbornly opinionated and outspoken.

Setting

An Old Testament "church" somewhere in the wilderness of Paran (Genesis 21:8-21). Pewlike bench or two chairs.

Lights up on pew. Deborah—dressed in Old Testament clothes but carrying a contemporary purse—enters and sits down. She looks around with reasonable interest. Anna enters on the opposite side of the stage, dressed in similar style to Deborah. She sees Deborah and sits down next to her. They are obviously friends.

ANNA	Good morning, Deborah.
DEBORAH	Hi, Anna. How are you this morning?

ANNA	Just fine. A little dusty. Our camel is on the fritz again. He's been kicking up a lot of sand. I think we're going to have to take him into the garage and have him checked. Mariah thinks he just needs a tuneup. I hope that's all it is.
DEBORAH	Be real careful. You can't trust most of the mechanics around here. They'll take a little one-hump job and before you know it, you're paying for an entire herd. (Beat) You look very nice today. Is that new?
ANNA	This? Are you kidding? Where would I get anything new around here on what we make? K-Mart won't open for another 3,000 years. I keep telling Mariah that he should quit that sheepherder's job, get back to night school, and qualify himself for something substantial. But does he listen to his wife? No. He says he likes working with sheep. He says they're quiet. What's that got to do with anything? (Points off to one side) Oh, look over there. Is that Gibeah?
DEBORAH	Yes, yes. I think it is.
ANNA	Who is that with her?
DEBORAH	I don't know. I've never seen him before.
ANNA	My word, she's in here every other week with someone new. I guess being a water girl can keep you pretty busy—if you know what I mean. Have you ever been to her house?
DEBORAH	No. Have you?
ANNA	She hosted a Tupperware party the other night. A housekeeper, she's not.
DEBORAH	When would she have time?
ANNA	She served some of the worst lamb-finger sandwiches I've ever had. It's no wonder she has so many different boyfriends. (Sighs) Well,

	you know what my mother used to say: "If you can't keep house, you can't keep kitchen; and if you can't keep kitchen—
BOTH TOGETHER	—you can't keep a man."
ANNA	It's true, it's true. She probably eats out a lot. (Pause, looks in another direction) Speaking of not keeping a man, look who just came in.
DEBORAH	It's Hagar.
ANNA	I wonder what she's doing here?
DEBORAH	I understand she's thinking of joining.
ANNA	She's not. She wouldn't have the nerve.
DEBORAH	Why not?
ANNA	You know she has that baby.
DEBORAH	I know. I thought it was from her deceased husband.
ANNA	No. Her husband is still living.
DEBORAH	He is? Then where is he?
ANNA	He's in Gerar. It's Abraham.
DEBORAH	Abraham! Oh, I've heard of him. Very powerful. What is she doing here?
ANNA	He threw her out.
DEBORAH	No kidding. Do you know why?
ANNA	I'm not sure of all the details but it had something to do with a conflict of inheritance with the sons or something like that. If you ask me, he just got tired of her. I mean, just look at the girl. Can you blame him? A fashion model she's not.
DEBORAH	But how did she get all the way here? That's a long distance for a woman and a child.
ANNA	I don't know. I heard Abraham gave her only a loaf of bread and some water.

DEBORAH	That's all? And she's still alive? I can't imagine how she did it.
ANNA	Sheer nerve. You know how those Egyptians are. Very persistent. Look at what they did with the pyramids.
DEBORAH	But look at her—she always seems so strong, so happy. I wonder what makes a woman like that tick? What keeps her going?
ANNA	It's sheer nerve, I told you.
DEBORAH	It must be more than that. Watch how she greets everyone. She acts like . . . like she belongs here.
ANNA	If she had any sense of decency, she wouldn't be here at all. Doesn't she know that there's a church down the road with a single-parent program? Why does she have to come here?
DEBORAH	Anna, you need to be more patient.
ANNA	It's disgusting. She has no pride.
DEBORAH	I just can't imagine how she does it. I think I'd be a wreck if Japheth deserted me with the kids. I'd never make it.
ANNA	Of course you would.
DEBORAH	I don't know how. What would I do? Who would I turn to?
ANNA	You silly girl, God'll take care of you. Haven't you been paying attention to your scriptures?
DEBORAH	I know God would take care of me, but . . . it would still be difficult.
ANNA	I'm here, Deborah. I'd help you.
DEBORAH	Would you, Anna? Really?
ANNA	Really. I would do that for you.
DEBORAH	Thank you. That's very nice of you. (Pauses) Ah . . . now I get it.

ANNA	Get what?
DEBORAH	Maybe God uses people to show his goodness to other people. Just like he shows his goodness to me through you.
ANNA	That's very profound.
DEBORAH	(Excited at her line of thinking) And . . . maybe God shows his goodness to Hagar the same way. Maybe that's what keeps her going.
ANNA	Yes and I'm sure the church down the road would be happy to have that opportunity.
DEBORAH	Anna . . .
ANNA	(Begins to stand) I think I'm going to powder my nose.
DEBORAH	Anna, if we would do it for each other, we should do it for her . . . shouldn't we?
ANNA	I'm sorry but I believe that's a principle to be introduced later on in the Bible. I want to keep my place. (She exits)
DEBORAH	(As she stands) Always a technicality, Anna. You always have a technicality. (She exits as well)

BLACKOUT (Curtain)

Discussion Questions

1. Read Genesis 21:8-21 to get some background for this sketch.

2. While this sketch is very speculative, what can we learn from Hagar's experience? What can we learn from Anna's and Deborah's attitudes throughout the sketch?

3. Deborah comes to a very significant conclusion toward the end of the sketch (which Anna doesn't seem to willing to accept). Is it a conclusion you agree with? If so, how can you make that conclusion work with some of the "outcasts" in your youth group? in your school?

Three Witnesses of Pentecost

I n this sketch we hear three separate eyewitness accounts of the day of Pentecost.

Characters

BARTHOLOMEW—A disciple.
URBANUS—A seller of rugs.
JOHN—A disciple.

Setting

A bare stage.

Full lights on stage. Bartholomew enters and moves casually to stage right as he speaks . . .

BARTHOLOMEW   Do I remember it? Are you kidding? How could I forget that day? Next to seeing our Lord physically risen from the dead, it was one of the most amazing things I've ever experienced. We were together in Jerusalem—we believers, that is—celebrating the Feast of Weeks. I'm sorry, you probably know it as Pentecost. Jews had

---

come from all over Israel, even the world, to be there. Anyway, I stray from the point. We were at Mark's, preparing to start off for the day's activities and suddenly it sounded like the wind was blowing. It was a violent sound, as if a storm were about to ravage the city, and it filled our ears until I thought they would burst. I looked up and there was fire all around. Not that anything was burning, the fire was just hanging in the air. It was beyond belief. This fire hung there and then slowly divided into smaller flames that moved above our heads. From that point, I . . . I don't have the words to describe the feeling . . . the *power.* Yes, I've thought about it a lot since then and I'd say power is a good word for it.

(Urbanus enters, moves center as he speaks)

URBANUS I came into town a couple of days before the feasts began—my wife and I. Hadn't been to Jerusalem in years. Years I tell you. Urbanus is my name, by the way, and I was selling rugs in Corinth back then but decided I hadn't been away for a long time and thought Jerusalem during the Passover would be great. Yeah, I know. Things were a little unsettled there what with the crucifixions and political unrest—but what do I care for such things? I was faithful to the ceremonies and sacrifices, I was a good Jew who worked hard and—can I confess it?—my *heart* wanted to go to Jerusalem. I'd been everywhere by then, all the big cities, but *that* city . . . oh, it had soul. So, there I was walking down the street with my wife and we wander right in the middle of this commotion. I thought the Romans were shaking someone up again but it was just a bunch of Galileans standing around shouting at the crowd. Normally, I wouldn't have thought that curious enough to stop because Galileans, as a rule,

don't impress me much. They're fairly unsophisticated, if you know what I mean. I figure
they're drunk, try to push on. But my wife is
tugging at my arm and I realize that these
Galileans are talking in a variety of different languages. Everybody—no matter where they were
from—understood these guys. Like I said,
Galileans are fairly unsophisticated. I've known
only a few who could complete a sentence in
their *own* language let alone *someone else's.* But
there they were and I was stopped in my tracks
and then one of them stood out from the rest
and spoke with such . . . such power about the
prophet Joel and a person called Jesus whom
they considered the Messiah.

(John enters, moves left as he speaks)

JOHN   Jesus told us it would happen. During our last
meal, before his arrest, He asked the Father to
send a Comforter to us. I am John. I was there.
And after he arose from the grave, he said we
must stay in Jerusalem until we were empow-
ered from on high. None of us were sure what
that meant—or what to expect. The last thing
we would have imagined would be to march
into the streets during one of our most holy
feasts, preaching in languages we had never
learned, risking arrest and possibly death at
the hands of those who tried to kill our Master.
We who ran at his arrest, cowered at his crucifixion, and doubted his resurrection were
proclaiming him in full view of the world
without fear or hesitation. Then Peter—oh, that
Peter—stood and preached. Loudly and boldly.
I knew Peter could be loud, but not quite so
bold. He repeated Joel's prophecy concerning
the outpouring of God's spirit on his people.
He proclaimed Jesus as both Messiah and resur-
rected Lord. He explained that all of them, like
us, were guilty of his crucifixion. By the power

URBANUS	of the Spirit he spoke and 3,000 were added to our number as believers.
URBANUS	My wife and myself were two of that number. Peter's words were strong. He indicted us all for having crucified the one sent from God. The Messiah. That day we took into our lives this strange new belief—the fulfillment of all we were as Jews. Shortly after that, I moved from Corinth to Rome, taking my faith with me to be shared there. I aided Paul from Tarsus—maybe you've heard of him?—I helped him in his work to start an assembly of believers there.
BARTHOLOMEW	And we devoted ourselves to teaching and to fellowship, to the breaking of bread and to prayer. We were all filled with awe, for many wonders and miracles were taking place among us. All of us stayed together and had everything in common as we sold our possessions and goods to give as each had need. And we continued to meet and proclaim Jesus in the temple courts and broke bread in various homes and ate together with glad and sincere hearts, praising God and enjoying the favor of all the people. And the Lord added to our number daily those who were being saved. Have I forgotten anything?
URBANUS	It's all written down in case you did.
JOHN	May the power work in you now as it did for us.

(Nodding their approval, they exit)

BLACKOUT (Curtain)

Discussion Questions

1. Imagine for a moment the scene described in Acts 2 and its impact on those present.

2. Imagine how you'd react if you were one of the people on the street. Why would you react that way?

3. How do you think most Christians would react now if such an event were to take place? Why would they react that way?

4. What impact do the happenings at Pentecost have on your life today? How can you spread the Good News beyond your immediate circle of friends?

Sketch 19

The Upper Room

I n this sketch we hear the conversation of Jesus and the disciples during their last meal together. The sketch is adapted from The New International Version of the Bible and various references regarding chronology. Use this sketch at a Good Friday service, communion service or whenever appropriate.

Characters

NARRATOR
JESUS
THE 12 DISCIPLES

Setting

A room where Jesus and the disciples are celebrating the Passover meal. Action can take place around a long table or reclining on the floor with cushions. As much or as little can be used for background sets as you desire. For the sake of authenticity, no lines or words have been added to what Jesus says. All of his dialogue comes from the Gospels as translated in the New International Version of the Bible. Important note: This sketch should be performed as normally and naturally as possible—without pretense or the self-conscious acting that often comes with portraying scriptural characters.

Before the lights come up, we hear the Narrator . . .

NARRATOR   The silver trumpets in the temple announced to all Jerusalem that the Passover had arrived. At that moment, Jesus and his disciples could be found reclining at a table in a small upper room. Here they—like all faithful Jews—would celebrate God's redemption of Israel from bondage to Egypt. But the Passover was more than that. It was also a time to look forward to the coming of the Lamb of God who would deliver Israel from bondage to sin.

Sadly, many did not realize that the Lamb of God was there among them, waiting for the plot to kill him to unfold.

Amidst the celebration and joy, it must have been difficult for the disciples to grasp that this would be their last meal with their Master before his arrest, trial and—finally—death on a cross. In this quiet upper room, thoughts of such horror and brutality must have been distant. Here, life went on as usual. The disciples, in all of their humanity, began to bicker and argue about which of them should have the places of prominence at the table. From that came a discussion of who among them would be considered the greatest in the coming kingdom. As he often did, Jesus had to teach them by an example. He—the Master—showed them how to be a servant by washing their feet.

(As the Narrator has been speaking, the lights have slowly come up on Jesus—who is washing John's feet with a bowl of water and cloth. The other disciples whose feet have been washed are reclining around a large table. The one end of the table—stage right—has an open seat. The head of the table has an open seat for Jesus. Next to him on his right sits John; on his left, Judas. Jesus reaches the final disciple—Peter)

PETER   (Pulling away) Lord, are you going to wash my feet?

JESUS   You do not realize now what I am doing, but later you will understand.

PETER   No. You shall never wash my feet.

JESUS   Unless I wash you, you have no part with me.

PETER   (Pausing to consider this, then speaks proudly)
                   Then, Lord . . . not just my feet but my hands and
                   my head as well!

JESUS   (Smiling patiently, washes Peter's feet and nothing
                   else. He stands and gestures for Peter to take the
                   seat at the far end of the table. Peter is not pleased
                   but obeys. Jesus speaks in a tone that is loving yet
                   clearly a rebuke of Peter's prideful attitude—and the
                   attitudes of the others) A person who has a bath
                   needs only to wash his feet; his whole body is
                   clean. And you are clean . . . though not every one
                   of you. (Jesus sets the bowl and cloth aside and
                   puts on his robe—as he continues to speak) Do you
                   understand what I have done for you? (He looks
                   around at them. A few look like they might try to
                   answer but don't; some continue to nibble and eat
                   the food on the table) You call me "Teacher" and
                   "Lord" and rightly so, for that is what I am. Now
                   that I, your Lord and Teacher, have washed your
                   feet, you also should wash one another's feet. I
                   have set you an example that you should do as I
                   have done for you. I tell you the truth, no servant
                   is greater than his master, nor is a messenger greater
                   than the one who sent him. Now that you know
                   these things, you will be blessed if you do them.
                   (He moves to the table, taking his position at the
                   head) I am not referring to all of you; I know those
                   I have chosen. But this is to fulfill the scripture:
                   "He who shares my bread has lifted up his heel
                   against me."

(The disciples react to this with confusion, conferring among
themselves)

JESUS   I am telling you now before it happens, so that
                   when it does happen you will believe that I am He.
                   I tell you the truth, whoever accepts anyone I send
                   accepts me; and whoever accepts me accepts the

one who sent me. (Long pause, the disciples quiet down and look to him) I tell you the truth, one of you is going to betray me.

(This causes an outburst from all—except Judas—as they cry out their allegiance to him, arguing, disputing and speculating with "Surely not I, Lord!" "This can't be!" "None of us would do such a thing!" "Who would do such a thing?" "I would never. How could you even think—" etc. Amidst this, Jesus stands casually with a bowl and bread and begins to walk around them. He continues speaking, but not with their full attention)

JESUS The one who has dipped his hand into the bowl with me will betray me. The Son of Man will go just as it is written about him. But woe to that man who betrays the Son of Man! It would be better for him if he had not been born. (He remains standing but has returned to his original position near Judas and John)

PETER (Calling to John, motioning) Ask him which one he means.

JOHN (Hesitates, rises to Jesus) Lord, who is it?

JESUS (To John alone, holds up piece of bread) It is the one to whom I will give this piece of bread when I have dipped it in the dish. (He dips the bread into the bowl and sits in his original position next to Judas. The disciples are still conversing and discussing as he does this. John remains standing, watching with apprehension. Jesus reaches out to give the piece of bread to Judas)

JUDAS (Who has been seated, looks at the bread, then to Jesus) Surely not I, Rabbi?

JESUS Yes, it is you.

(Judas takes the piece of bread, looks at it)

JESUS What you are about to do, do quickly.

(Judas puts the bread in his mouth, turns and exits hastily. The disciples—noticing Judas' departure—react with confusion and speculation)

NATHANIEL	What has happened? Where is he going?
THOMAS	Is he going for more food?
JAMES	The Master must have sent him to give to the poor. Their need seems so great before the Feast.
JESUS	Now is the Son of Man glorified and God is glorified in him. My children, I will be with you only a little longer. You will look for me, and just as I told the Jews, so I tell you now: Where I am going, you cannot come. A new commandment I give you: Love one another. As I have loved you, so you must love one another. All men will know that you are my disciples, if you love one another.
PETER	Lord, where are you going?
JESUS	Where I am going, you cannot follow now, but you will follow later.
PETER	Lord, why can't I follow you now? I will lay down my life for you!
JESUS	Simon, Simon, Satan has asked to sift you as wheat. But I have prayed for you, Simon, that your faith may not fail. And when you have turned back, strengthen your brothers.
PETER	Lord, I am ready to go with you to prison and to death!
JESUS	I tell you, Peter, before the rooster crows today, you will deny three times that you know me. (He turns to them all reassuringly) Do not let your hearts be troubled. Trust in God; trust also in me. In my Father's house are many rooms; if it were not so, I would have told you. I am going there to prepare a place for you. And if I go and prepare a place for you, I will come back and take you to be with me that you also may be where I am. You know the way to the place where I am going.
THOMAS	Lord, we don't know where you are going, so how can we know the way?

JESUS I am the way and the truth and the life. No one comes to the Father except through me. If you really knew me, you would know my Father as well. From now on, you do know him and have seen him.

PHILIP Lord, show us the Father and that will be enough for us.

JESUS Don't you know me, Philip, even after I have been among you such a long time? Anyone who has seen me has seen the Father. How can you say "Show us the Father"? Don't you believe that I am in the Father, and that the Father is in me? Rather, it is the Father, living in me, who is doing his work. Believe me when I say that I am in the Father and the Father is in me; or at least believe on the evidence of the miracles themselves. I tell you the truth, anyone who has faith in me will do what I have been doing. He will do even greater things than these, because I am going to the Father. And I will do whatever you ask in my name, so that the Son may bring glory to the Father. You may ask me for anything in my name, and I will do it If you love me, you will obey what I command.

NARRATOR Jesus continued to teach them . . . of the Holy Spirit who would come to guide them and comfort them. He spoke of his return and assured them of the special place they would have as his followers. And then he took bread and wine to institute a special memorial . . .

JESUS I have eagerly desired to eat this Passover with you before I suffer. For I tell you, I will not eat it again until it finds fulfillment in the Kingdom of God. (He takes a jar, gives thanks silently, then speaks) Take this and divide it among you. For I tell you I will not drink again of the fruit of the vine until the Kingdom of God comes. (He fills his cup then picks up the bread, give thanks silently for it, then breaks it) This is my body given for you; do this in remembrance of me. (He passes the bread to them and they pull off a piece to eat. As they do, he lifts up his cup) This cup is the new covenant in my blood, which is poured out for you. (He passes the cup and they each drink. He continues to speak as they drink) Peace I leave with you; my peace I give to you. I do not give to you as the world gives. Do not let your hearts be troubled and do not be afraid . . . Come now, let us leave. (He stands, moves to exit. They follow accordingly, offstage)

NARRATOR When they had sung a hymn, they went to the Mount of Olives . . . And from there, history would change its course, and all eternity would ring with the echo of a hammer against spikes and a stone being rolled away . . .

(Congregational hymn appropriate to this moment and the occasion in general)

Discussion Questions

1. How does this sketch of the Last Supper differ from other accounts you've seen or read? How is it similar?

2. Read the accounts in the Gospels of this event. (Matthew 26:17-30; Mark 14:12-26; Luke 22:7-39; John 13—17.) How are the accounts similar? different? What parts speak to you personally the most?

3. What does communion mean to you?

4. Which of the disciples can you most identify with? Why? How would you have reacted to Jesus' words if you were present at the Last Supper?

5. When Jesus washed his disciples' feet, he was demonstrating the role of a servant. How can you be a servant to friends in need? new kids at school? new members at church or youth group? your family? others in your community?

Sketch 20

Women's Missionary Fellowship

(Thanks to Jeremiah People for this one.)

I n this sketch we join three ladies discussing the recent visit of a missionary at their church and how "generous" it would be if they got "financially" involved.

Characters

TAMMY—A haughty, gossipy type who is more concerned about her own full stomach than others.
TERI—Similar to Tammy's character. Loves to eat.
VICKI—Not particularly intelligent. Could be played with a heavy nasal quality in her voice.

Setting

Any kind of meeting place. Three chairs.

Lights up on the three women seated next to one another.

TAMMY   (Licking her fingers) Ummm-ummh. This icing is just heavenly. I've got to get this recipe.

VICKI   Oh, I know! My husband says I gain five pounds every time I come here to Missionary Fellowship.

TERI	(Joking) Oh, you know, I'm just a naughty girl having all these calories.
VICKI	But calories taste so good!
TERI	Well, I figure the Lord wouldn't have given me a stomach if he didn't want me to fill it. (Chuckles, pause, eating)
TAMMY	What did you girls think of our speaker today?
VICKI	Oh, better than average, I'd say. At least she didn't bring any of those leprosy slides like Miss Peutabach did last month. (Groans, showing disapproval on her face) Things like that certainly take the edge off my appetite.
TAMMY	You know, I've never even heard of E.T. Opium . . . or whatever you call it.
VICKI	That's *Ethiopia*.
TAMMY	Oh, right . . . Until today.
VICKI	I heard it on the news one morning.

(At this point, Teri, with a mouthful of pecan pie, turns to Vicki, indicating that something is caught in her teeth. During Tammy's next line, which neither of them hear, Vicki mimes to Teri, "What's stuck in your tooth?")

TAMMY	What was it she said they always ate over there?
TERI	(Responding to Vicki's question) Pecan, I think.
TAMMY	(Surprised) Pecan?!
TERI	(Turning to Tammy) Yeah . . . (Pointing) . . . right there in my tooth. (Puts her finger in her mouth and picks) Ah! Got it!
TAMMY	Wasn't it rice?
VICKI	In pecan pie?
TAMMY	No, in E.T. Opia. That's what it was she said they always ate, wasn't it?
TERI	You wouldn't catch my Herbie only eating rice . . . it's

meat and potatoes or I never hear the end of it.

VICKI   Well, maybe rice has something in it we don't know about.

TAMMY   Could be. Well, anyway, it was real informative. (Leans in and lowers voice) Although I did think she dressed a little . . . shabbily.

TERI   (Low) Oh, honey, did you see those shoes that she was wearing? They look like the ones my grandmother wore for 10 years and then gave to the Salvation Army.

TERI   Speaking of starvation . . . (To Vicki) . . . would you be a dear and pass me another fudge brownie, please?

(Vicki mimes passing a plate which she takes from an imaginary table next to her. Teri takes a brownie and Vicki puts the plate back)

TERI   Oh, thank you. (Takes a big bite)

BLACKOUT (Curtain)

Discussion Questions

1. What points are made by this sketch?

2. What are your thoughts about "indulgences" of the flesh—particularly where eating is concerned? Is there anything in scripture about overeating? If so, what does it say?

3. What do you agree with or disagree with about the attitudes of the women toward those less fortunate? While we may not say so outwardly, do you think their attitudes are representative of a lot of people's thinking? yours? Explain.

4. How can you and your youth group reach out and support missionaries? Ask your pastor to help you think of ideas; for example, collect canned goods, clothing or money and send them to missionaries or world relief programs.

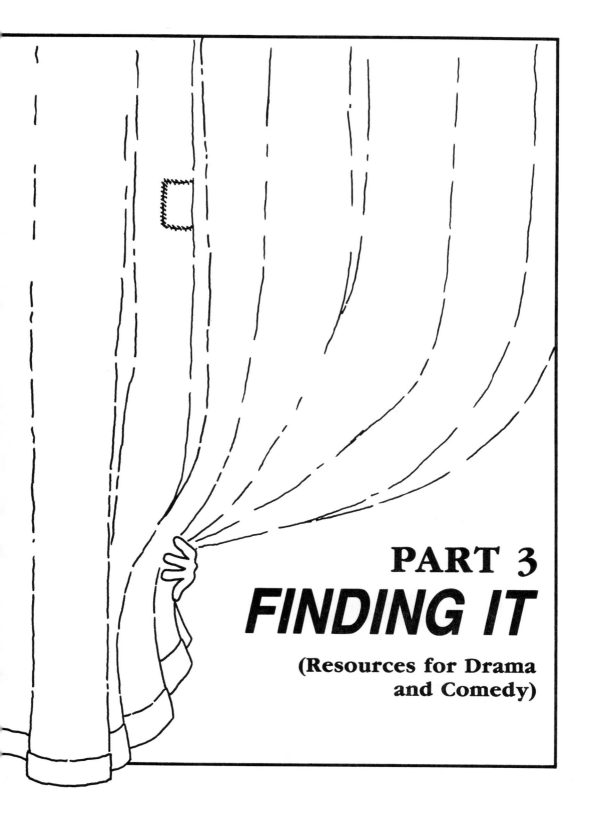

PART 3
FINDING IT
(Resources for Drama and Comedy)

Play List (Compiled by Deborah Craig-Claar)

Group 1: Plays by Major Playwrights With Direct Christian Themes

These plays identify human beings as experiencing a self examination of their own finiteness and their relationship with God. Many of these plays cover forgiveness, repentance, atonement, judgment, confession and faith. Christ is clearly recognized as the Son of God and Redeemer of humanity.

All of the plays in this listing can be ordered through your local bookstore. Or you can find many of them in a local city library or university library.

Anderson, Maxwell:
Both Your Houses
Joan of Lorraine
Journey to Jerusalem
Winterset

Anonymous:
Everyman
Wakefield Mystery Plays
(especially *The Second Shepherds' Play*)
(Any of the *Medieval Mystery, Miracle* or *Morality* plays; secure a modernized version)

Anouilh, Jean:
Becket
The Lark

Benet, Stephen Vincent:
A Child Is Born

Chayefsky, Paddy:
Gideon

Coxe, Louis & Chapman, Robert:
Billy Budd

Dunsany, Lord:
Plays of Gods and Men

Eliot, T.S.:
Murder in the Cathedral
The Family Reunion

Fry, Christopher:
The Boy With a Cart
The Firstborn
A Sleep of Prisoners

Green, Paul:
In Abraham's Bosom
The Lord's Will

MacLeish, Archibald:
J. B.

Marlowe, Christopher:
Doctor Faustus

Maeterlinck, Maurice:
Mary Magdalene

Mansfield, John:
The Coming of Christ
Good Friday
Easter
The Trial of Jesus

Miller, Arthur:
The Crucible

Osborne, John:
Luther

Shaw, George Bernard:
Androcles and the Lion
Saint Joan

Tolstoy, Leo:
The Power of Darkness

Group 2: Plays by Major Playwrights With Implied Christian Themes

Although these plays do not address biblical subjects or events directly, they are written to engage the audience in a self-examination for meaning in their own lives.

Anderson, Robert:
I Never Sang for My Father

Barry, Philip:
John
You and I

Beckett, Samuel:
Endgame

Benet, Stephen Vincent:
John Brown's Body
(dramatized version)

Bolt, Robert:
Man for All Seasons

Connelly, Marcus:
The Green Pastures

Crothers, Rachel:
Susan and God

Davis, Ossie:
Purlie Victorious

Eliot, T.S.:
The Cocktail Party

Goodrich, Frances & Hackett, Albert:
The Diary of Anne Frank

Hansberry, Lorraine:
A Raisin in the Sun

Howard, Sidney Coe:
The Silver Cord

Ibsen, Henrik:
Ghosts
The Master Builder
Brand

Lawrence, Jerome & Lee, Robert E.:
Inherit the Wind

Levy, Benn:
The Devil Passes

Masters, Edgar L.:
Spoon River Anthology
(dramatized version)

McCullers, Carson:
The Member of the Wedding

Miller, Arthur:
Death of a Salesman

Nash, Richard:
The Rainmaker

Odets, Clifford:
Awake and Sing

O'Neill, Eugene:
The Iceman Cometh
Mourning Becomes Electra

Shakespeare, William:
King Lear
Macbeth
Othello
The Tempest

Steinbeck, John:
Of Mice and Men

Strindberg, August:
The Ghost Sonata

Wilder, Thornton:
Our Town
The Skin of Our Teeth

Group 3: Christian Drama

These plays address biblical characters, events or themes. They are written with a direct Christian perspective and are often intended expressly for church production. Most of the cast requirements and publishing houses are included.

Arden, John:
Serjeant Musgrave's Dance (13M/4W, Methuen)

Arden, John & D'Arcy Margaretta:
The Business of Good Government: A Christmas Play (10M/4W, Methuen)

Auden, W.H.:
For the Time Being (A Christmas oratorio, Random House)

Baird, John:
The York Nativity (15M/2W, French or Baker's Plays)

Berryhill, Elizabeth:
Cup of Trembling (6M/2W, Seabury)

Bloch, John:
Armour of Light (3M/4W, Bethany Press)

Bolte, Chuck & Shippy, Dennis:
Jeremiah People, Sketchbooks: Volumes I-V (Five separate volumes of sketches. Thousand Oaks, CA: Jeremiah People, 1980-1984)

Brock, James:
Modern Chancel Dramas, five plays:
The Witness
And Such a King
The Human Condition
The Last Days
A Sound From Heaven
(Baker's Plays)

Brocket, Henri:
Christmas at the Crossroads (3M/4W, McKay)

Carlino, Lewis John:
The Brick and the Rose (7M/3W, Dramatists Play Service)

Carroll, Paul V.:
Shadow and Substance (6M/3W, Dramatists Play Service)

Coffee, Lenore & Cowen, William:
Family Portrait (12M/10W, Samuel French)

Forsyth, James:
Emanuel (LARGE cast, Theatre Arts)

Gheon, Henri:
Christmas on the Village Square (LARGE cast, Samuel French)

Gheon, Henri (cont.):
The Journey of Three Kings
(8M/1W, Baker's Plays)
The Way of the Cross
(5M/3W, Baker's Plays)

Hartman, Olov:
Mary's Quest (7M/7W,
Baker's Plays)

Johnson, Albert:
The People vs. Christ
(2M/1W, Baker's Plays)

Kennedy, Charles:
The Servant in the House
(5M/2W, Baker's Plays)

Kliewer, Warren:
The Prodigal Son (3M,
Golden Quill)

LeRoy, Warner:
Between Two Thieves
(9M/4W, Baker's Plays)

Mankowitz, Wolf:
It Should Happen to a Dog
(2M, Baker's Plays)

**McCusker, Paul &
Albritton, Tim:**
A Small Concoction (A
Broadway-style musical
comedy. Unpublished.
Available from author.)
*The Meaning of Life &
Other Vanities* (4M/4W,
Baker's Plays)

**McCusker, Paul &
Smith, Herb:**
A Family Christmas
(2M/4W/Extras, Contem-
porary Drama Service)

McCusker, Paul:
Batteries Not Included (A
collection, Baker's Plays)
*The Case of the Frozen
Saints* (7M/2W, Baker's
Plays)
Catacombs (10M/3W,
Lillenas)

McCusker, Paul (cont.):
*The First Church of Pete's
Garage* (6M/5W, Baker's
Plays)
Home for Christmas
(2M/3W, Baker's Plays)
Sketches of Harvest (A col-
lection, Baker's Plays)
Souvenirs (A collection,
Baker's Plays)
Vantage Points (A collec-
tion, Lillenas)
The Waiting Room
(4M/3W/6 non-gender,
Baker's Plays)

Mueller, Don:
Eyes Upon the Cross (8
different plays, Baker's
Plays)

Nemerov, Howard:
Cain (4M/1W, Univ. of
Chicago)

Nicholson, Norman:
Birth by Drowning
(8M/5W, Faber & Faber)

Obey, Andre:
Noah (5M/4W, Samuel
French)

Rutenborn, Guenter:
The Sign of Jonah (8M/3W,
Thomas Nelson)

Schevill, James:
The Bloody Tenet
(10M/1W, Meridian)

Schnieder, Patricia:
*Crossroad to Bethlehem
Peter* (Baker's Plays)

Swann, Darius:
The Circle Beyond Fear
(12 people, Friendship
Press)

Turner, P.W.:
Christ in the Concrete City
(4M/2W, Baker's Plays)
Cantata for Derelicts
(4M/2W, United Church
Publishing)

Turner, P.W. (cont.):
*Cry Dawn in Dark
Babylon* (4M/4W,
Baker's Plays)

Vane, Sutton:
Outward Bound (6M/3W,
Samuel French)

Ward, R.H.:
The Builders (4M/1W,
Baker's Plays)

Ward, R.H. (cont.):
The Prodigal Son (4M/2W,
Baker's Plays)

Williams, Charles:
Grab and Grace (4M/2W,
Oxford University Press)
House by the Stable
(4M/2W, Oxford Univer-
sity Press)

Additional Reading

Besides reading *Youth Ministry Drama and Comedy* there
are other books and resources that will help you start
comedy and drama in your church. Here are some resources we
recommend.

Background and History

Brockett, Oscar G.:
History of the Theatre,
fourth edition (Boston:
Allyn & Bacon, 1968).

Overall Production/Directing

Allensworth, Carl:
*The Complete Play Pro-
duction Handbook*,
revised edition (New
York: Harper & Row,
1982).

Miller, Dan:
The Production Organizer
(Newbury Park, CA: DSM
Associates, 1985). Avail-
able from the author:
3847 San Clemente,
Newbury Park, CA 91320.

Morrison, Hugh:
Directing in the Theatre
(New York: Theatre Arts,
1974).

Sievers, W. David et al.:
Directing for the Theatre,
third edition (Dubuque:
Wm. C. Brown, 1974).

Tompkins, Dorothy Lee:
*Handbook for Theatrical
Apprentices* (New York:
Samuel French, 1983).

Plays and Other Material

Baker, George Pierce:
Dramatic Technique,
reprint of 1919 edition
(Brooklyn: Greenwood,
n.d.).

Grebanier, Bernard:
*Playwriting: How to Write
for the Theatre* (New
York: Harper & Row,
1979).

Acting

Boleslavski, Richard:
*Acting: The First Six
Lessons* (New York:
Theatre Arts, 1949).

Kahan, Stanley:
Introduction to Acting
(Boston: Allyn & Bacon,
1985).

Morris, Eric:
Being & Doing (New York:
Perigee Books, 1981).
Irreverent Acting (New
York: Perigee Books,
1985).

**Morris, Eric &
Hotchkis, Joan:**
No Acting, Please (New
York: Perigee Books,
1979).

Stanislavski, Constantin,
Actor Prepares (New York:
Theatre Arts, 1948).
Building a Character (New
York: Theatre Arts,
1977).

Voice and Speech

Anderson, Virgil A.:
*Training the Speaking
Voice* (New York:
Oxford University Press,
1977).

Davis, Ken:
*How to Speak to Youth . . .
and Keep Them Awake
at the Same Time*
(Loveland, CO: Group
Publishing, 1986).

Makeup, Lights, Sound and Set Construction

Baygan, Lee:
*Make-Up for Theatre, Film
& Television* (New York:
Drama Book, 1982).

Corson, Richard:
Stage Make-Up (Old
Tappan, N.J.: Appleton-
Century-Crofts, 1986).

Reid, Francis:
Stage Lighting Handbook
(New York: Theatre Arts,
1976).

**Rosenthal, Jean &
Wertenbaker, Lael:**
The Magic of Light
(Boston: Little, 1972).

Drama Publishers and Organizations

C ontact these organizations for sketches, plays, acting exercises and other general drama needs.

Plays/Sketches/Musicals

Baker's Plays
100 Chauncy St.
Boston, MA 02111

Broadman Press
127 Ninth Ave. N.
Nashville, TN 37234

I.E. Clark Inc.
St. Johns Road
Schulenburg, TX 78956

Contemporary Drama Service
Box 7710
Colorado Springs, CO 80933

The Drama Book Publishers
Box 816
Gracie Station
New York, NY 10028

Dramatists Play Service
440 Park Ave. S.
New York, NY 10016

Dramatic Publishing Company
311 Washington St.
Woodstock, IL 60098

Samuel French Inc.
45 W. 25th St.
New York, NY 10010
 or
7623 Sunset Blvd.
Hollywood, CA 90046

Group Publishing
Box 481
Loveland, CO 80539

Jeremiah People
Box 1996
Thousand Oaks, CA 91360

Lillenas Publishing
2923 Troost
Kansas City, MO 64109

Paul McCusker
Box 1996
Thousand Oaks, CA 91360

StorySource
119 N. Hite
Louisville, KY 40206

Youth Specialties
1224 Greenfield Drive
El Cajon, CA 92021

Children's Plays

(Some children's plays can be obtained from the previously listed companies also.)

Anchorage Press
Box 8067
New Orleans, LA 70182

Coach House Press Inc.
Box 458
Morton Grove, IL 60053

Plays Inc.
120 Boylston St.
Boston, MA 02116

Melodramas

(Some melodramas can be obtained from the previously listed companies also.)

Pioneer Drama Service
2172 S. Colorado Blvd.
Denver, CO 80222

Periodicals

Church Drama Ideas
Box 1861
Arvada, CO 80001-1861

Lillenas Drama Newsletter
2923 Troost
Kansas City, MO 64109

Theatre Crafts Magazine
135 Fifth Ave.
New York, NY 10010-7193

Drama Book Clubs

The Fireside Theatre
501 Franklin Ave.
Garden City, NY 11530

Lighting

Altman Stage Lighting
57 Alexander
Yonkers, NY 10701

Art Craft Theatre Equipment
517 W. 35th
New York, NY 10001

Grand Stage Lighting
630 W. Lake St.
Chicago, IL 60606

Little Stage Lighting
Box 20211
Dallas, TX 75220

Kliegl Bros. Inc.
5 Ariel Way
Syosset, NY 11791-5502
    or
15720 Ventura Blvd.,
Suite #607
Encino, CA 91436

Olesen Theatrical Supplies
& Lighting
Box 438
Hollywood, CA 90078

Strand-Century Lighting
5432 W. 102nd St.
Los Angeles, CA 90045

Sound

Sound Investment
Enterprises
Box 4139
Thousand Oaks, CA 91359

F & H Entertainment
2144 N. Lincoln Park W.
Chicago, IL 60614

HME (Remote Systems)
9675 Business Park Ave.
San Diego, CA 92131

Masque Sound
331 51st St.
New York, NY 10019

Nady Systems
1145 65th St.
Oakland, CA 94608

Vega Electronics
9900 Baldwin Place
El Monte, CA 91731

Effects

The Dramatists Play
Service
440 Park Ave. S.
New York, NY 10016

Special Effects
Unlimited
752 N. Cahuenga Blvd.
Hollywood, CA 90038

Theatre Production
Service
59 Fourth Ave.
New York, NY 10003

Promotion

Package Publicity
Service
27 W. 24th St.
New York, NY 10010

Costumes

American Costume
Company
1526 Blake St.
Denver, CO 80202

Atlanta Costume
Company
2089 Monroe Dr.
Atlanta, GA 30324

Brooks-Van Horn
 Costume Company
117 W. 17th St.
New York, NY 10011

Eaves Costume
 Company
21-07 41st Ave.
Long Island City, NY 11101

Hooker-Howe Costume
 Company
4652 S. Main St.
Bradford, MS 01830

Krause Costumes
1660 E. 40th St.
Cleveland, OH 44103

Salt Lake Costume
 Company
1701 S. 11th St.
Salt Lake City, UT 84105

Texas Costume Company
2607 Ross Ave.
Dallas, TX 75201

Western Costume
 Company
5335 Melrose Ave.
Los Angeles, CA 90038

Makeup

Bob Kelly Cosmetics
151 W. 46th St.
New York, NY 10036

Max Factor
1666 N. Highland Ave.
Hollywood, CA 90028

Ben Nye Company
11571 Santa Monica Blvd.
Los Angeles, CA 90025

Stein Cosmetic Company
430 Broome St.
New York, NY 10013

Scenery

Peter Albrecht
 Corporation
325 E. Chicago St.
Milwaukee, WI 53202

J.C. Hansen Company
423 W. 43rd St.
New York, NY 10036

Secoa
1204 Oakland Ave.
Greensboro, NC 27403

Texas Scenic Company
Box 680008
San Antonio, TX 76268

ADD FUN TO YOUR MINISTRY...

CLOWN MINISTRY

Floyd Shaffer and Penne Sewall

Discover how to touch lives as a Christian clown! You'll explore practical tips for...

- developing a clown character,
- mime techniques,
- makeup and costumes, and
- interpreting the Bible.

Plus, you'll get 30 detailed skits and more than 50 brief clowning activities to cover a variety of topics, including...

- forgiveness,
- world hunger,
- stewardship,
- pride,
- reconciliation,
- family,

...and more—including unity, Christ's passion, and loneliness. Use this book to bring the excitement and fun of clown ministry into your church today!

ISBN 0-936664-18-5

CLOWN MINISTRY SKITS FOR ALL SEASONS

Floyd Shaffer

You'll find dozens of imaginative skits to mark special occasions, including...

- Christmas—Share a "hobo" meal and remember the true meaning of the season,
- Birthdays—"Bake" a giant cake using spiritual ingredients,
- Easter—Distribute Easter eggs with crosses inside,
- Valentine's Day—Share God's love,
- Retirement—Throw a "movin' on" party, and
- Thanksgiving—Give yourself to God in thanks.

Whether you're part of a clown ministry troupe or work solo, you'll find skits that fit your style. Use these routines for...

- worship,
- service projects,
- fellowship times,
- youth group events,
- outreach,
- holiday celebrations,

...and other special occasions. This one-of-a-kind collection of clown skits will help you lead your church in uplifting celebrations throughout the year.

ISBN 1-55945-053-3

Order today from your local Christian bookstore, or write: Group Publishing, Box 485, Loveland, CO 80539. For mail orders, please add postage/handling of $4 for orders up to $15, $5 for orders of $15.01+. Colorado residents add 3% sales tax.

EASY-TO-DO SKITS BRING LIFE TO YOUR GROUP

SHORT SKITS FOR YOUTH MINISTRY

Draw your kids into discussions with more than dry lectures. Each skit packs a significant punch on such teen-friendly topics as...

- sharing faith,
- money,
- marriage,
- world hunger,
- parents,
- nagging,
- sibling rivalry,
- time management.

And each skit is simple to prepare. Assign the parts and let kids create their own characters on the spot. After you've opened the topic for discussion with a skit, use the questions provided to help kids uncover biblical truths on important issues.

Skits are ideal for almost anywhere and for any time. There are no special set requirements—rather, skits use props you already have, such as chairs or a park bench if you're outdoors.

Use these skits to involve kids in growing closer to God.

ISBN 1-55945-173-4

FUN GROUP-INVOLVING SKITS

Use these quick, no-rehearsal dramas as opening crowdbreakers, short devotionals, or to introduce a theme for a whole meeting. Skits are based on familiar Bible stories such as...

- David and Goliath,
- Creation,
- Jonah and the big fish,

...and topics such as...

- peer pressure,
- sexuality,
- fears,

...and many more, all in a variety of pantomime and acting situations. There's no memorization needed, and each skit is followed by discussion and follow-up activities.

ISBN 1-55945-152-1

Order today from your local Christian bookstore, or write: Group Publishing, Box 485, Loveland, CO 80539. For mail orders, please add postage/handling of $4 for orders up to $15, $5 for orders of $15.01+. Colorado residents add 3% sales tax.